Stopmotion Explosion

Stopmotion Explosion

Animate ANYTHING and Make MOVIES

How to make epic films using everyday stuff

Check out the free downloads and additional resources online!

www.stopmotionexplosion.com

Stopmotion Explosion
PO Box 967, North Dighton, MA 02764

Third Edition, Revised: June. 2017

ISBN 978-0-9833311-3-1

Computers : Digital Media - Video & Animation
Performing Arts : Animation
Performing Arts : Film & Video - Amateur Production

Chapter layout and design by Jeff Flynn
Storyboard (page 62) & Fight Arc (page 152) illustrations by Mark Eckerson

*Dedicated to my parents and siblings
for their never-ending support
and my filmmaking mentors*

Contents

Chapter 1

Horse Hooves, Paintings, and How Movies Work

Today, almost anyone can get their hands on a video camera. Cameras are embedded in phones and laptop screens, hidden in watches, cars, and stuffed animals, and very affordable (compared to the first primitive camcorders, which would set you back a few thousand bucks in today's inflated dollars).

Because the world is so saturated with video, somewhere along the line we've forgotten how fundamentally weird this moving-image phenomenon is. We just accept it. But now stop a moment and think. You're watching a picture that moves. Sometimes the things you see happened a long time ago, or somewhere far away. You're there, but you're not there. That's pretty weird.

If you're watching an animated Pixar film, or playing a video game, you're looking at places and people that don't even exist. It's like you're peeking inside someone's imagination.

Stop-motion animation is a filmmaking technique that blends the real world with the illusion of video in a new way, and makes video weird again. It's like seeing an elephant disappear off a stage. Your head knows someone is tricking you, but your eyes are screaming "Holy cow! That was AWESOME".

Stop motion makes familiar objects do unexpected things, and video becomes magical again. For some, this weirdness is a mental block to understanding how stopmotion works, because they think they understand how movies work:

"Movies show moving things moving."

Is this true? Sometimes.

Wires? Greenscreen? CGI?

When toys and other stuff come to life in a movie today, the audience assumes the creators used special effects, invisible wires, computerized 3D models, or erased their fingers out of the video using the greenscreen stuff. You might think the same.

As you'll discover in this book, basic stopmotion is much simpler and uses none of the techniques above. In fact, stopmotion has been in existence almost as long as the medium of film!

The key to understanding stopmotion is understanding what movies really are, and how they trick our eyes into seeing motion. To help you understand how this is possible, let's take a trip through movie history.

A Short History of Film

Before the photograph was invented, artists captured the world around them in sketches, pastels, oils, and other mediums. Horses were strong, beautiful subjects, but artists could never agree about one thing. Did all four of a horse's hooves leave the ground during a gallop? Jean Louis Théodore Géricault thought they did, and he painted *The Epsom Derby* this way in 1821.

The Epsom Derby, (1821)

Photography was invented in the early 1800s. The process used a flat surface covered with chemicals that changed colors when exposed to light. One of the first photographs was made by artist Joseph Nicéphore Niépce in 1827. It's a picturesque image of a barn roof and some walls; the view from his window. The camera had to sit in the window for eight hours before an image was traced in the photographic chemicals by the sun. It was some time before the chemical formulas improved, and photos could capture a moving object without the image blurring into mush.

One of the first photographs, made by Joseph Nicéphore Niépce, (1827)

Inventors were making progress in other fields. In London during the 1820s it was discovered that painting two images, one on each side of a card, suspending the card between two strings and spinning the card rapidly would combine the images into one. The toy was named Thaumatrope, from the Greek for "wonder turner." It's very easy to make a Thaumatrope. Can you invent a design of your own?

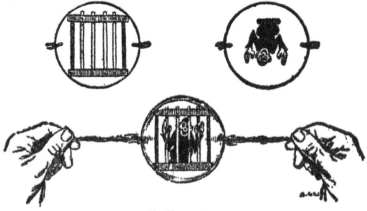

The Thaumatrope

The Zoetrope

Roughly ten years later, the Zoetrope was invented. Several pictures of an object in motion were printed on a strip of paper and placed inside a circular drum with slits cut in the sides. By spinning the drum and looking through the slits, the viewer saw a flickering, looping image that appeared to move. The name "Zoetrope" is derived from the Greek for "wheel of life." Today, we call this illusion of movement "Persistence of Vision."

Muybridge's famous horse sequence

Artists were still debating horses. In 1872, Leland Stanford, former governor of California, horse racing man and railroad tycoon made a bet with photographer Eadweard Muybridge intending to answer the question forever. Do all four hooves of a galloping horse leave the ground at once?

Muybridge placed several cameras around a racetrack, stretching wires attached to the cameras' shutters across the horse's path. As the horse galloped past, the wires broke, triggering each camera in succession.

The series of pictures proved that all four hooves do leave the ground. History was made, Muybridge won the bet, and artists, including Edgar Degas studied the images closely, using them to improve their paintings and sculptures.

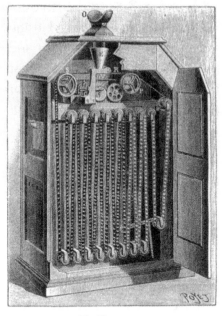

The Kinetoscope

In 1889, Thomas Edison was given a roll of George Eastman's newly invented flexible photographic film. Edison had seen Muybridge's work and was developing a moving picture device in collaboration with Edison Labs photographer William Dickson. Edison saw how a long row of pictures printed on the new film could be shown to a viewer, one picture at a time, using a system of rollers, a crank, and a peephole in the top of a box. As the viewer turned the crank and looked into the box, the pictures flashing past appeared to move, thanks to the persistence of vision effect discovered by inventors of the Thaumatrope and Zoetrope.

Le cinématographe Lumière: projection.

The Cinématographe in projector mode. Note the hand-turned crank feeding a spool of film in front of the light. The light source, a bright arc lamp, is focused on the film with a series of lenses. The light passes through the transparent film, projecting the image onto a screen. (Mustache optional.)

This device, which Edison named the Kinetoscope, became very popular. Audiences lined up outside Kinetoscope parlors, and George Eastman's Kodak film became the basis of a whole new moving picture industry.

In 1895 the Lumière Brothers, Aguste and Louis, revealed their Cinématographe, a device that captured a series of images on a strip of film, developed the film, then projected the image on a screen by shining a bright light through the clear film. This was the first modern film projector.

Edison followed this invention with the Vitascope, the first commercially successful projector in the United States. This was the beginning of the movie theater industry as we know it today.

Humorous Phases of Funny Faces, (1906)

A strip of film. Each picture is one "frame."

Stop-motion

In 1896, James Stuart Blackton was experimenting with the stop-action movie technique. It was a simple way to create basic special effects. The camera would record a portion of film, then stop. Everyone froze in place while an actor ran off screen. After the actor disappeared, the camera restarted and the remaining actors pretended to be amazed. To the audience sitting in the theater, it looked like the actor had suddenly vanished.

While reviewing footage of an outdoor scene where the camera had been started and stopped several times, Blackton noticed clouds drifting across the background looked funny. He decided to replicate the comic effect in new films. Eventually, he discovered that starting and stopping the camera in very small increments, one picture or "frame" at a time and moving an object while the camera was stopped created the illusion of motion.

One of Blackton's first films created with this technique: *Humorous Phases of Funny Faces* (1906) was a series of chalk drawings on a blackboard. Between frames, Blackton erased, or added a new lines to the drawings, creating characters that smiled, blinked, and smoked cigars.

Puppet Animation

Blackton progressed to creating short films with small puppets. The puppet was moved in little increments. Each time the puppet moved, a picture was taken of its new position.

King Kong, (1933). He's a lot tamer when you realize all that gorilla muscle is a bunch of rubber and rabbit fur, about 18 inches high. This said, Kong is more than a match for a rubber pterodactyl!

Stopmotion puppets can be very complex. Skeletons, called armatures, are made out of thin, flexible materials. Wire, or rods of metal ending in ball joints and special connectors are used. Clay, foam, rubber, fabric, and other materials are wrapped around this skeleton, until it looks like a character.

In the US, movies with hand-drawn animation (like Blackton's *Humorous Phases*) became more popular than stopmotion using puppets. Stopmotion became a technique used mainly to create special effects in live-action films. The work of Willis O'Brien, an early effects animator, can be seen in movies like *King Kong* (1933). The rise of stopmotion's popularity can been seen in early TV shows for kids. *Gumby* (1953) and *Davey and Goliath* (1960) are two examples your parents may be familiar with (clips of all these films can be found on YouTube.)

Stopmotion films remain popular today. Movies like *Wallace and Gromit: The Curse of the Were Rabbit* (2005), *Chicken Run* (2000), *Fantastic Mr. Fox* (2009), and others have proved audiences' taste for the unique look and storytelling opportunities that stopmotion offers. Additionally, many people are discovering the simplicity and flexibility of stopmotion while creating movies with their own computers and cameras. That's what this book is about!

A Word about Computers

You'll be running video and image editing programs. These require more memory and resources than a text editor, but your system does not need to have the specs of a supercomputer. Here are the recommended computer requirements.

Windows Minimum Requirements

- **Operating System**: Windows XP SP3 +
- **Processor**: 1 GHz, recommended: 1.5 GHz or higher
- **Memory**: 512 MB of RAM minimum, recommended 1 GB or higher
- **Hard Disk**: 2.0 GB of available space, 10 GB recommended
- **Video input**: USB 2.0, FireWire required for digital camcorders

Apple Minimum Requirements

- **Operating System**: Mac OS X 10.7+
- **QuickTime** 7.1 or later
- **Processor:** Intel core processor
- **Memory**: 1 GB or more RAM recommended
- **Hard Disk:** 2.0 GB
- **Video input**: USB 2.0, FireWire required for digital camcorders

Note that these are the minimum requirements, and animating or editing HD video will require more processing power. Upgrading your computer, or using a better laptop will make your work faster and more enjoyable.

Stopmotion Explosion

Chapter 2

Animation Actors

cquiring an eye for animated movement takes time and practice. It's best to begin animating simple objects, like a small rubber ball, a green plastic army man, or the kind of stuff lying on top your desk. One of my favorite beginner materials is a lump of Silly Putty®.

You can animate the putty rolling around the table, changing shapes, and climbing over things.

Add a couple of googly eyes for extra character.

Introducing: The Minifig!

I have an affinity for films made with toys, particularly LEGO® bricks and minifigs. A professional, all-metal stop-motion armature can cost upwards of $300 dollars. If you're a stop-motion newbie with $300 to burn, I'd advise spending half of that amount on LEGO®, and the rest building your stop-motion setup. You will have much more to work with.

You can buy minifigs for a few dollars each. Buying a LEGO® set, gives you a complete movie location to film, or vehicle for your new actors to drive. You can even buy minifigs and LEGO® sets based on TV shows and movies, like Indiana Jones, Star Wars™ and The Lord of the Rings™.

Minifigs have 7 movable joints, which is a nice middle ground between complex, many-jointed armatures (King Kong) and jointless toys

(green army men). Minifig heads are available with many facial expressions, which allow your characters to show a range of emotions. The studs on a LEGO® baseplate are a great way to measure and limit minifig movements, particularly while creating walking or running animations. You'll quickly appreciate the way a minifig sticks to the baseplate without toppling over.

Minifigs are the putty monster's favorite food!

Introducing: ModiBot Mo!

ModiBots are another small inexpensive super-poseable figure with interchangeable parts and accessories. ModiBots have been designed in a way that makes them perfect for animating.

A basic ModiBot Mo figure has three joints in the arms and legs, a waist joint, and neck joint, for a total of 14 points of articulation. Compared to the seven joints LEGO® minifigs have, ModiBots are a great way to increase the complexity and realism of your animations.

It can be tricky to balance a ModiBot, particularly if you're animating a walk or run cycle, but a small piece of clear tape is usually enough to restore his equilibrium. I've also successfully inserted small magnets into the bottom of his feet for balancing on a magnetic whiteboard surface, and figured out how to use screw-in tie downs for more stability. Tie downs will be introduced later in this chapter. For the magnetic project, and other ModiBot experiments, visit the *StopmotionExplosion.com* blog.

CHECK IT OUT!

On the Blog: Magnetic Modibot

stopmotionexplosion.com/magnetic-modibot

ModiBots can be painted, sanded, drilled, and combined with other ModiBot sets, allowing the creation of many different characters. What makes Mo unique among many other toys is the ability to 3D print amazing new parts and accessories from the BotShop. More information about this can be found on the **Modibot.com** website.

Throughout this book you will also see pictures of ModiBot Mo's distant cousin, a smaller figure called a Stikfa. These were made by a separate company and are no-longer being manufactured, but are still available from some sellers. Like the ModiBot, they are a fun, slightly more advanced figure to animate.

ModiBots, Stikfas and LEGO® minifigs are just two of many toys, models and figures that can star in an animated film. Look for jointed figures that hold a pose, are easy to balance and adjust, and come with accessories that can be used as props.

ModiBot Mo with his trusty Venture Kit, and on the right, his ninja Stikfa buddy.

PROJECT

Building an Armature

The Skinny on Armatures

Figures constructed around armatures have a long history in the stopmotion world. As I mentioned previously, they can be expensive. A complex, custom-made, machined-metal armature can cost upwards of four figures. Kit-based armatures cost less, but are still expensive, running around $150 to $300 each. If you'd like to build your own armature, it would be best to start with a wire and epoxy putty model, as pictured here. These are cheap and fairly simple to make.

The wire used in this armature is heavy gauge aluminum wire. It's flexible, light, and strong, but has a tendency to break if nicked, so be careful while forming your figure.

The "bones" of the armature are made of epoxy putty, a material that can be purchased at most hardware stores. The putty prevents the wire from becoming unwound and gives the figure joints, allowing repeatable, restricted movement like a real person.

The body of the figure can be bulked up with clay, foam, cotton, or latex. If you measure the limbs and torso so that the figure stands 12" tall, you can dress it in clothes made for 1:6 action figures (such as G.I. Joe ™).

Finally, the feet of the armature are threaded, allowing the figure to be screwed down to a table surface while animating.

Want to start animating with an armature? Follow these step-by-step instructions and roll your own. Kids, get assistance from an adult first!

PROJECT

Armature Materials

- 16-18 gauge aluminum wire
- Epoxy* putty
- Epoxy* glue
- Small piece of 3/4" plywood

> *Please be sure to read and follow all manufacturers' safety warnings before using epoxy products.*

Aluminum wire can be inexpensively purchased online. If you're a scavenger type, scrapped aluminum wire can be found inside heavy-duty electrical wiring, the kind strung between poles (NOT the stuff inside your walls!) Use thinner wire for smaller armatures.

Tie down Materials

Tie downs are the mechanism used to fasten the armature to the table while you animate. You'll need the following. Make sure the nuts match the screw thread you're using!

- 2 x 10-32 machine screws, or piece of 10-24 threaded rod
- 2 x small nuts, no more than 3/8" in diameter
- 2 x wing nuts

Tools

- Handheld electric drill
- Drill bits: 5/32", 1/4" & 3/8"
- Vise
- Pliers
- Wire cutters

The Steps

1 Cut off a four foot section of wire. Bend the wire in the middle so the two ends meet. Stick the bent end into the bit holder of an electric drill. Tighten the bit holder until the wire is held fast. Clamp the two loose wire ends in a vise. Pull the wire straight, and run the drill slowly. The two strands of wire should twist together.

PROJECT

2 Using wire cutters and pliers, form the twisted wire into the shapes pictured here. Wrap the wires together into the shape of your figure.

3 Cut two 3/4" x 1-1/2" pieces of plywood. Drill a hole halfway through one end of the first piece of wood, about where the wire is inserted in the opposite picture. The size of your drill bit should be large enough so that your twisted wire fits snugly inside the hole (try 5/32").

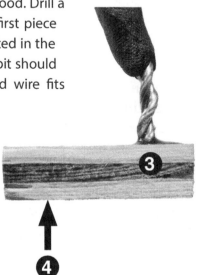

4 Drill a second, 1/4" hole completely through the other end of the wood, where the arrow is in the photo. This hole will be used as a pilot hole for the next step.

5 Using the 3/8" bit, drill a hole halfway through the bottom of the foot. Mix a small amount of your epoxy putty following the instructions on the container, and insert the putty into the hole. You can use a small amount of epoxy glue instead, but you'll have to be very careful to not get it inside the nut threads in the following step!

2 *Wire figure shape*

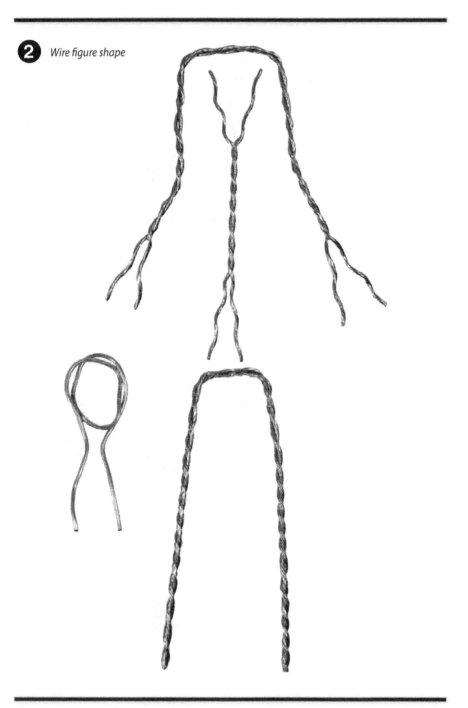

6 Insert one of your small nuts into the bottom of the foot. Be careful to not get any glue or putty inside the nut threads. One way to avoid this is by inserting the screw into the nut before sticking the nut into the foot, as pictured here.

7 Repeat this process for the other foot and allow the putty or glue to harden. If the nut ever pops out, superglue is a good way to re-anchor it into the foot.

8 Mix together more epoxy putty, and form the "bones" of your armature. Allow the putty to harden.

9 Dip the two wire "legs" of the armature into epoxy glue and insert into the two half-drilled 5/32" holes. Apply more glue as needed. Allow the glue to dry.

Instead of creating wooden feet for your armature, you can simply create two loops of wire in the ends of your armature's legs, insert the bolts inside these loops, and epoxy glue them into place. You can then drill a hole in the bottom of a shoe or boot created for a 1:6 scale doll, and stick your armature's leg inside. Or, you can mold a shoe around the foot with clay.

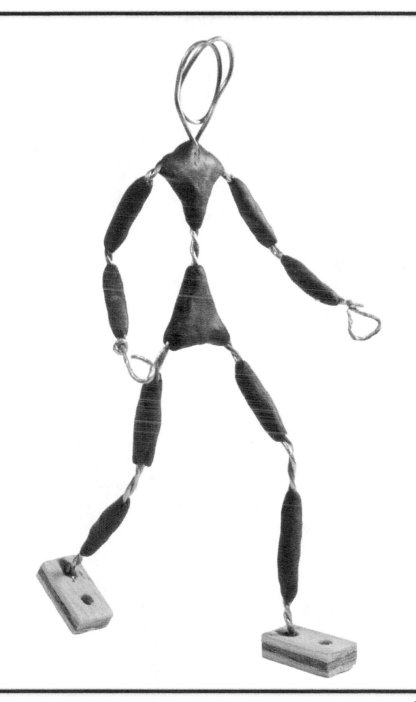

Pegboard Table Animation

While waiting for the glue to dry, you can start making your tie downs. For me, this was simple as using a hacksaw to remove the heads from a couple of 10-32 machine screws. If you have a piece of threaded rod, cut it into two short lengths. These pieces, used in combination with the wing nuts, will be screwed into the armature's foot and used to anchor it to the animation table's surface.

You can also work on a surface for animating with your new armature. I raided a pile of scrap wood and came up with enough pieces to make a very simple table, the top of which is made from 1" pegboard,

the kind used for hanging tools. Instead of making a floor-standing table, make a table that can be placed on top of another table.

The table pictured is 2' high. This will allow you to reach underneath and adjust your tie downs easily.

To use the armature with the tie downs, screw one end of a tie down into the armature foot, insert the other end into a pegboard hole, and snug it tight with a wing nut underneath. This is why you want the underside of your table to be easily accessible. Bending over constantly to adjust your tie dows is a real pain (in the back!)

With one foot anchored, your armature can pose in all sorts of crazy positions without falling over.

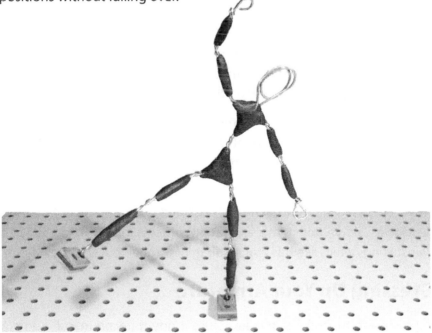

Modibot Mods

Interestingly, it's possible to screw a #10 diameter machine screw into the foot of a ModiBot. The plastic is soft enough that the screw will thread the foot by itself. This allows you to use a pegboard table and tie downs to practice ModiBot animation.

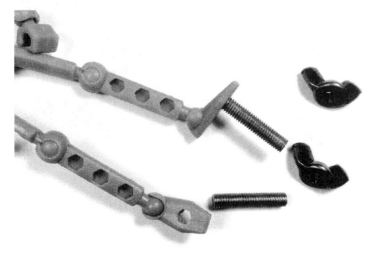

If you watch a stopmotion feature film, or any professionally made animation, you'll quickly notice that they do not animate on pegboard surfaces. If this is the case, how do they use tie downs?

The answer is simple. Every time the figure needs to be anchored to the table, a hole is drilled into the table surface with a handheld drill. After the armature's foot comes up again, the hole is filled with clay, and a new hole is drilled somewhere else.

This process of drilling and filling up holes, and fastening and unfastening tie downs slows down the animation process down a lot, but it's painstaking details like this that result in high-quality stopmotion films.

Dressing Up Your Armature

If you want to bulk-up the armature body, I recommend using a combination of sports prewrap foam, and self-grip athletic tape. Both

Self-grip tape on the left, and sports pre-wrap on the right

can be purchased at your local pharmacy. If you use just the foam, be prepared to add a layer of tape over it to hold it in place. The self grip tape can hold both itself, and a layer of foam in place, as you can see in the picture.

These materials are much cleaner than clay if you plan to dress up the armature in 1:6 doll clothes!

Other Methods

Most of the animating techniques I cover in this book apply to puppet and object animation. Other forms of stopmotion also exist.

Papermation

Sometimes called "cutout animation," papermation is made with flat materials. The camera is suspended directly above a table, pointing downward. Photos, newspaper and magazine cutouts, characters made from card stock, construction paper and so forth are placed on the table and animated.

A cutout animation can be enhanced by drawing on the table surface around the cutouts, similar to the method James Blackton used to animate *Humorous Phases of Funny Faces*. To give a very simple example, if you animated a car pulling away from a stop sign, you could draw some skid marks and a cloud of dust behind it.

HOW TO

Animate a Rocket Engine

This cutout rocket, made with sissors, construction paper, gluesticks, and markers has three stages of construction-paper rocket-engine power!

When the rocket is going fast, the largest stage is placed on the end. When the rocket is decending slowly into a lunar crater, the smallest stage is used.

With a little cotton wool spread beneath the rocket, "smoke" caused by the rocket exhaust can be animated. Liftoff!

Feel free to trace and copy the rocket for use in your own projects. Or create a design of your own!

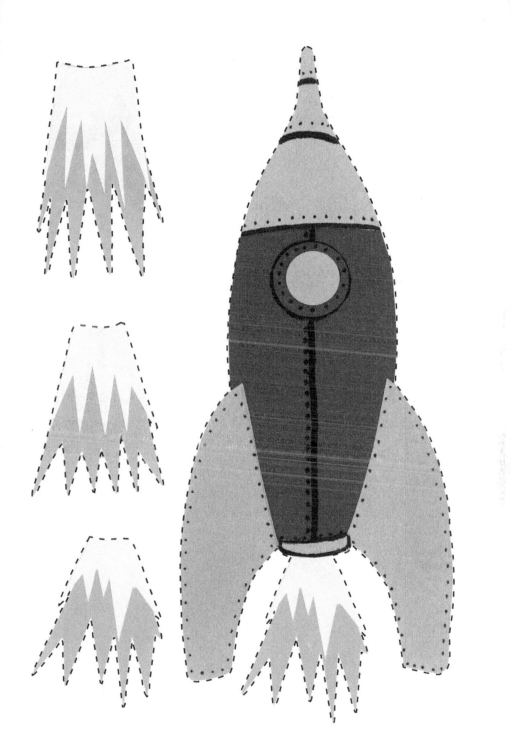

Overhead Camera Mount

You can pick up an inexpensive microphone stand for around $20-40 dollars. These make great, flexible small-camera mounts when working with cutouts or a light box.

In this example, a small webcamera has been attached to the end of the stand with a bunch of rubber bands.

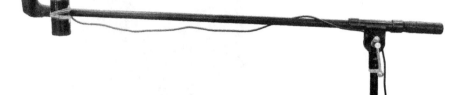

Sand & Paint Animation

Sand animations are made on top of a "light box" (a shallow box topped with a semi-opaque material, like frosted glass or paper) that allows diffused light to pass through.

This light box was built with four pieces of scrap plywood and sheets of waxed paper stretched tightly across the top. If you're planning to

animate a lot of material on top of a light box, purchase a square piece of white Plexiglas and use it in place of the paper in this example. Plexiglas is durable, easy to work on and clean, and the white Plexiglas diffuses the light nicely.

As with paper animation, a camera is positioned over the box pointing downwards. Sand is visible as a black shadow on top of the light box. The sand is animated by pushing it into new shapes. Any fine-grained material can be used in place of sand. Try kitty litter, bird seed, or fine-grained pasta. A paintbrush is handy for brushing the sand across the top of the box.

Paint animation is very similar. Slow-drying oil paint is spread and animated on a glass surface. A light box with a glass top can be used for paint animation.

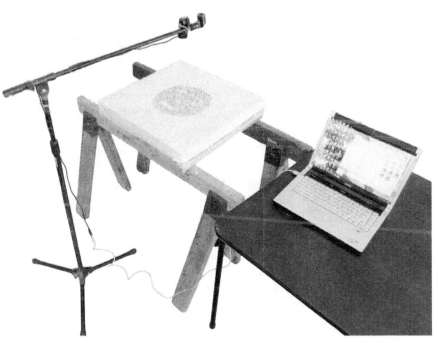

Simple light box setup. The light source (a scoop lamp, as pictured in the Lighting chapter) is placed on the floor, under the light box. The light box is resting on a couple of sawhorses.

People Animation

People can act as a living armature, moving one frame at a time in sync with the camera. Interacting with your animated characters is a one application of this technique. You could animate a giant hand reaching into a scene and grabbing something, or being attacked by a mob of plastic green army men.

As mentioned in the example box here, you can animate entire films by poising people and immobile objects. Chair races anyone?

HOW TO

Make someone float

If you have a digital camera, check to see if it has a "sports" setting, used to photograph action without the picture blurring.

Photograph someone jumping into the air repeatedly. Take pictures when the person is at the top of their jump, knees tucked under them. After jumping, the subject should walk forward one step and jump again.

String the photos together (either flip through the pictures using the camera's image preview, or use a program that converts pictures into video. Check out the Frame Conversion chapter).

If done correctly, it will look like the person is hovering around the yard, knees under them.

Chapter 3

Creating Stories

[T-Rex chasing a jeep driven by ninjas!]

Your first animations will probably be random doodles, lacking any plot or story structure. This is natural, as you're learning the basics of stopmotion; camera angles, frame rates, timing, lighting, set construction, and T-Rex diets.

Eventually, you'll want to move beyond doodling and start applying your new skills creating bigger and better projects.

I believe animators have an advantage over the average *"Hey-man! I-got-a-camera-let's-make-a-movie!"* filmmaker. This person grabs their friends, invents a story on the fly, and edits the footage together in an afternoon. Only his friends and mom care about the result.

In contrast, even a poorly made stop motion film is interesting to watch, because the filming technique itself is unique. Secondly, instead of a filmmaking style based around constant improvisation, animators are forced to think before they start filming. They visualize the footage needed, then create and animate according to this "mental movie" in their head. Since unused or mis-animated clips represent hundreds of frames of wasted work, the animator is trained to visualize thoroughly and efficiently. Both animators and live-action filmmakers need this skill.

In this chapter, I'll show you how to develop your "mental movies" into easily understandable forms that can be used to improve and share your story with other people.

Writing

You may be dismayed to learn that crafting movies requires writing skillz.

Lest you turn to the good ole' excuse: *"I don't need to write anything! It's all in my head!"*, there are many reasons why you should get your story on paper in some form before you start animating.

The Basics

The process of visualizing and planning a film before shooting is called "pre-production." Writing a screenplay is the first part of pre-production.

Short films are great practice for longer projects, and more likely to be watched all the way to the end when posted on video sharing sites, like YouTube. You should be thinking about stories that can be told in two to five minutes.

Writer #1 - "I have no story ideas"

Here are a bunch of ideas to jump start your right-sided creative brain.

Adaptation

Adapt a short story, or chapter of a book you like. This could be a couple of paragraphs, a short incident, or a "gag" that made you laugh. There are many comics and memes that could be adopted into short animations.

Comic Adaptation

Adapt a scene from a comic book. It's already storyboarded (more on storyboards to come!)

Movie Adaptation

Find a screenplay for a film that you've never seen, but are interested in watching (many are available at IMSDB.com). Animate a scene from the screenplay. Then watch the real thing. How does your adaptation measure up to the original?

The Joke

Re-tell a silly joke in movie format. *"Two ropes walk into a..."*

Based on a True Story

Animate something based on a life experience, humorous or otherwise.

School Exercise

Instead of writing a paper for school, present the subject as a short movie. (Get permission from your teacher first.)

Mashup

Get your storyteller juices flowing by mashing existing stories, characters and places together.

Character #1 goes to **Location** and meets **Character #2**

becomes...

King Kong goes to **New York** and meets **The Mario Bros**.

Writer #2 - "I have ideas!"

Perhaps you're one of those naturally gifted individuals to whom writer's block is completely unknown *(yeah right)*. Great. Let's start writing!

Sum up your idea in a few short sentences. If you have several ideas, write them all down. You can use pencil and paper, or a computer, whatever feels more natural. If you're not sold on a particular story idea, it may be possible to combine pieces of several ideas into one story. Listing ideas will help you better see what fits together.

After you've outlined the story idea in a paragraph or two, and are happy with the concept, it's time to start working on the screenplay.

The Power of Adjectives

Good stories are built around characters with flaws. Often, the flaws move the story forward. For example, a character may want something badly, but this reward is impossible to obtain until their personal flaws are overcome.

Describing characters with adjectives is a great way to begin defining their personality. Below, I've underlined the adjectives describing characters, along with a goal each character is trying to accomplish.

- *"__Shy__ politician collects votes"*
- *"__Clumsy__ beaver builds a dam in his peaceful woodland community"*
- *"__Lackadaisical__ secretary transcribes complex reports"*
- *"__Aquaphobic__ life-guard saves baby dolphin"*
- *"__Loud__ drill sergeant takes job as substitute librarian"*
- *"__Timid__ cowboy crosses the Mohave desert... alone"*

A hero with a personality that hinders their desires, or hijacks their quest is a great foundation to build a story on, since the character's journey to achieve their goal is an uphill battle the moment they step out the front door.

Asking questions about a character is a great way to begin laying the framework of a story. For example, the drill-sergeant turned temporary librarian:

- Why is a drill-sergeant working at the library? Is the regular librarian sick?
- Does the librarian greet people loudly when they walk in the door? Do they shout when books are returned late?
- How to the library visitors react?
- Does the librarian learn that their loudness is having a bad effect on visitors?
- Does a situation arise that allows the librarian to use their loudness for good? What other skills does a drill-sergeant have?
- How does the librarian regain the trust of the patrons?

People you know may provide material for your character's personality. Do you know any loud people? How would they behave if they became a librarian for the day?

Before writing a long screenplay, writers often develop an extended description of the story, called a "treatment", that outlines the entire story start to finish. Since we're developing a very short film, our paragraph-long description will serve as the treatment. From the treatment, we will write the screenplay.

Spec Scripts and Shooting Scripts

Spec scripts are written by enterprising screenwriters hoping to sell their story to a producer. They contain the film's story and dialog, and not much else. Shooting scripts are much more detailed, and are used by the crew and director while the film is in production.

Properly written screenplays follow a number of formatting and spacing rules. Instead of fussing with margins and fonts, it's easier to use software that automatically formats your text as you type. I list a few of these programs at the end of the chapter, and explore the features of Celtx, a free open-source program.

I'll start by creating a screenplay in spec script format, then convert the screenplay into a shooting script. You don't have to complete these two steps if you'd rather focus on other aspects of filmmaking, but I hope the information in the rest of this chapter may be of use to you someday.

Use a screenwriting program, like Celtx as you apply the techniques in this section (download links at the end of the chapter).

CHECK IT OUT!

Script Example

Here are a couple of pages from the spec-formatted screenplay for *Jack Spelt and the Sandstone Caves*, a short LEGO® film used as an example throughout this book

Jack Spelt Shooting Screenplay

6.

EXT. GRANDPA SPELT'S HOUSE - NIGHT

                    PIRATE CAPTAIN
          Harr Harr! The map is MINE

The Pirate Captain shoots through the smashed window,
extinguishing the light inside. The world returns to
darkness.

EXT. GRANDPA SPELT'S HOUSE - MORNING

Early morning passerby stare at the kicked-in gate and
window, now shuttered tightly.

INT. GRANDPA SPELT'S HOUSE - MORNING

Grandpa Spelt is seated at his desk. The large painting has
been returned to its place.

                    GRANDPA SPELT
          You must go to the cave and recover
          the treasure before the pirates
          steal it. You are the only living
          descendant and will receive the
          treasure when I die.

Grandpa Spelt wheezes, stressed from the night's ordeal.

JACK SPELT, young, rugged, listens attentively. He scratches
his head.

                    JACK SPELT
          After extensive consideration and
          analysis of the facts available,
          I've concluded my progress will be
          hindered without a map.

                    GRANDPA SPELT
          Precisely my boy, which is why I'm
          giving you this.

Grandpa Spelt reaches under his desk and brings out an MP3
RECORDER.

Jack Spelt rises and stares at the gadget.

                    JACK SPELT
          A digital music player? I've always
          wanted one of those. But.. how on
          earth is it going to help me get
          the treasure?

                                          (CONTINUED)

```
                    GRANDPA SPELT
               I've placed an audio tour of the
               sandstone caves on here that will
               guide you to the hiding place of
               the treasure.

He lays the recorder on the table.

                    JACK SPELT
               Umm... OK... if you say so.

                    GRANDPA SPELT
               Good luck my boy.

Jack takes the recorder from the table and EXITS the room.
```

• • • • • • • • • • • • • • • • •

Master Scene Format

Screenplays written in Master Scene format are composed of three parts. **Scene Headers**, **Description**, and **Dialog**. One page of screenplay written in this format is equal to (roughly) a minute of film. So, a 120 page screenplay is a 120 minute feature film.

All screenplays are written in 12pt `Courier` font. Screenplays start with the words `FADE IN:` and end with `FADE OUT.` (Hollywood sez! No exceptions).

Scene Headers

What's a scene? If you check out the Jack Spelt screenplay in this chapter, you'll see three separate scenes. Scenes are a way to divide a story into smaller chunks. They are created when the story moves to a new location, or a long period of time passes. Headers are used to mark the beginning of scenes.

Headers or "slug lines" contain three pieces of information, abbreviated as the three **W**'s. **W**hether, **W**here and **W**hat:

1 Whether the location is exterior, abbreviated: EXT. or interior, abbreviated: INT.

2 Where the action occurs, for example: BILLY JOE'S GOAT FARM or NEW YORK SUBWAY.

3 What time the action occurs, either: DAY, NIGHT, MORNING, or EVENING.

The last element, time is separated from the first two header elements by spaces and a hyphen. Put it all together and you get this formula:

```
EXT. / INT. LOCATION - TIME OF DAY.
```

You'll need to create a new header each time the location or time changes. For example, if a character inside a subway moves outside, the header needs to change:

```
INT. NEW YORK SUBWAY - NIGHT
```

becomes:

```
EXT. NEW YORK STREET - NIGHT
```

You can also use LATER, if the location remains the same:

```
EXT. NEW YORK STREET - LATER
```

We'll revisit scene headers when we convert our spec script into a shooting script.

Description / Action

The description starts below each scene heading. This is the story within the script, containing actions, visuals, sounds and characters.

Action is always written in the present tense:

```
Sally walks to the window
```

Past tense is never used:

```
Sally walked to the window (WRONG!)
```

Avoid flowery descriptions. Keep your paragraphs short and sweet. Describe only what is necessary to tell the story.

Write only what can been seen and heard. Emotions, such as *"Fred feels happy"* is non-visual and cannot be seen, but *"Fred smiles"* is a visual emotion that communicates his feelings. Non-visual events, such as thoughts and memories can be shown in flashbacks, dialog, or actions that reveal a character's mind.

Break long paragraphs of action into smaller paragraphs. Starting a new paragraph is a great way to suggest a new camera angle.

Several elements in the action should be written in capitals. This will assist the process of making a shooting script, as the capitalized elements are easier to pick out of the rest of the text. The first two rules are the most important and should always be followed.

 Capitalize all letters of a speaking character's name when they appear for the first time. After this, you may type their name using normal capitalization:

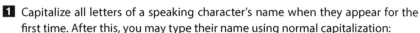

JOE, 40s, wearing suit and dark shades

2 Capitalize ENTERS and EXITS when used in context of a character entering and exiting a scene:

Joe ENTERS the gas station.

3 Capitalize important props and vehicles:

Joe reaches for the SHOVEL

4 Capitalize sounds that are essential to telling the story, and will needed to be added afterwards. You don't have to capitalize environmental sounds, such as birds chirping, or doors slamming, unless these contribute to the story in some way.

Joe sits in the chair. It CREAKS loudly and collapses.

Dialog Blocks

These are the conversations in the film. If you look at the Jack Spelt script, you'll see a bunch of them. Dialog blocks, sometimes called "speeches" are composed of three parts:

Character Name	BOB
Parentheticals (wrlys)	(to Jordan)
Dialog	More the merrier, I say!

The **character name** is always capitalized.

Parentheticals are also called **wrylys**, (named after the bad screenwriting habit of using (wryly) to describe the tone of a character's comment). Parentheticals state how dialog should be said: (loudly), (excitedly) and so forth, when tone isn't immediately apparent from the script.

Wrylys should also be used is when a group of characters is present, and the writer needs to clarify who the speaker is addressing. Otherwise, avoid using parentheticals.

Dialog follows the character name and any parentheticals. If the dialog is off-screen (maybe the character is in another room) the abbreviation (O.S.) is typed after the character's name:

JOE (O.S.)

What came in the mail?

If a character is narrating in a voice over (say they're recalling a past event and it's playing on the screen as they describe what happened), the abbreviation (V.O.) is used.

SGT. FRIDAY (V.O.)

I picked the kid up on a 903. Case closed, or
so I figured.

Improving Dialog

Writing dialog that doesn't feel fake is challenging. Much technique can be learned by listening to conversations between real people, paying attention to dialog in films you enjoy, and reading screenplays.

As you write, test the dialog by saying your characters' lines out loud. If they sound canned, it's a good indication that something needs to change. Would you say the same thing if you were in your character's shoes?

Reading your screenplay out loud is a good way to time the length of the movie it will become (use a stopwatch). If your voice actors are available, you can invite them to read their parts, and adjust accordingly.

I have passed over some more obscure terms and conventions that screenwriters use. You can learn much more about screenwriting through resources available online, and at your local library.

HEADS UP

Warning!

You are moving into advanced screenwriting territory. These techniques are best suited for big, complicated productions, and might be overkill for a small project.

Celtx

Celtx, the open-source screenwriting program is extremely easy to use. Fire it up and click *Film* in the *Project Templates* splash screen.

The main Celtx window appears. At the bottom of the window, click the *Tile Page* tab.

Video Tutorial: Using Celtx

stopmotionexplosion.com/screenwriting

| Script | TypeSet/PDF | Scratchpad | Index Cards | Title Page | Reports |

Fill in the *Title, Author, Copyright* and *Contact Information* fields. If your story is based on an existing work, fill in the *Based On* field too.

Switch back to the *Script* tab. If you look at the upper left corner, you'll see the words *Scene Heading* in a drop-down menu. Click this menu, and select *Text*.

Type FADE IN: all caps. Hit *ENTER* on your keyboard.

Click the drop-down menu again, and click *Scene Heading*, or hit *SHIFT + TAB*. Type out your first scene heading, following the rules I've outlined in this chapter.

Hit the *ENTER* key again, and you'll notice the drop-down menu changes to *Action*. Type in some action, again following the conventions I've outlined in this chapter.

When you're ready to type your first block of dialog, click *Character* in the drop-down menu, or hit *TAB*. Type in the character's name, and hit *ENTER*. The drop-down menu will switch to *Dialog*. Type your dialog lines and hit *ENTER*. Celtx will switch back to *Character*.

- To switch back and forth between *Scene Header* and *Action* mode, hit *SHIFT + TAB*.
- To switch to *Character* and *Dialog* mode, hit *TAB*.

There are several additional modes in the drop-down menu, including *Parentheticals*.

As you type, you'll notice little bars appearing under the text, containing character names and other script elements. This is Celtx's autocomplete feature! Hit **ENTER** to insert Celtx's suggestions into your text.

Drafts

After typing FADE OUT. the first draft of the screenplay is complete. Print a few copies and let your friends read it. Ask for their opinion.

Honest opinions can be difficult to find. If your friends think your feelings will be hurt if they criticize something you've written, it's OK to be vague about the script's authorship.

As a writer, you have to be open to a reader's critique. While criticism may seem like a personal attack, view it as an opportunity to improve your work. Respond correctly. If readers have difficultly understanding a plot element, don't say *"It will make sense in the movie!"* or *"You poor mortals cannot comprehend my genius!"* Revisit the element, introduce it earlier in the script, or cut it out entirely if it doesn't work (often the best choice!) Do whatever it takes to improve your story.

After you've incorporated your readers' input into the screenplay, you've completed the second draft.

And now, it's time to step away. Set the screenplay on a shelf somewhere and forget about it. After a period of self-imposed separation, pick up the screenplay and edit ruthlessly. This is your third draft, and may be the final, if it passes another round of readers with better success than the first draft.

You can continue writing drafts forever. The cycle stops only when you weigh the pros of continued edits against the cons of never shooting the film.

As a new writer/director, you're gaining a wide range of skills, not all of which involve writing. The visual aspects of storytelling are best learned through practical experience. Don't let an endless series of drafts separate you from shooting the film, an experience that will teach you many things which can be applied when you write the next screenplay. There will always be a next time.

Shooting Scripts

After your screenplay has undergone much tweaking, readings, and drafts, you're ready to start shooting. It's time to create a shooting script.

The format of a shooting script allows several people, each playing a different role in the production, to easily extract and organize information relevant to their job. It also allows changes in the script to be tracked and distributed in a way that keeps everyone on the same page. For the lone animator, a shooting script provides a great organizational system for storyboards and video files created during the animation process.

The steps required to create a shooting script are simple.

1. The pages of the screenplay are numbered.
2. The scene headers are numbered.
3. The script is LOCKED and labeled with a Revision Color.

Locking the Script

Scripts are locked when you're sure no major changes will be made, other people are coming alongside you to assist with the project, and (of course) you're ready to start shooting.

Simply put, locking a script means setting scene and page numbers in stone. They will never change again. Scene 1 will always be Scene 1. Page 6 will always remain Page 6 and so on.

This prevents a lot of confusion. If the director decides to add a couple of pages between the hero's dramatic entrance on Page 6 and the epic duel on Page 7, a edit that moves Page 7 ahead to Page 9, everyone's notes about the *"epic duel on Page 7"* will be wrong, resulting in mass panic, wasted work, or worse.

Editing Locked Scripts

New pages, and new scenes are inserted into a script with a letter after the scene or page number.

A scene inserted between 6 and 7 would become scene 6A. Additional scenes would be labeled 6B, 6C and so on.

Pages inserted between page 11 and 12 would become page 11A, 11B, 11C... etc.

Asterisks (*) are placed next to the scene header, and each line of changed text on each changed page. If you compare the locked Jack Spelt script with the unlocked version, you'll notice one of these changes.

Finally, the revision color and date of the revision is placed in the header of every page. If a scene is removed from the script, the header and action is deleted and OMITTED is written next to the scene number.

68   OMITTED

Script Example

This is a page from *Jack Spelt and the Sandstone Caves*, after being locked and formatted as a shooting script. See if you can spot the revision, marked with an asterisk (*).

Jack Spelt Shooting Screenplay

Blue Revision - 02-11-09   6.

9   EXT. GRANDPA SPELT'S HOUSE - NIGHT

                       PIRATE CAPTAIN
                Harr Harr! The map is MINE

        The Pirate Captain shoots through the smashed window,
        extinguishing the light inside. The world returns to
        darkness.

10   EXT. GRANDPA SPELT'S HOUSE - MORNING

        Early morning passerby stare at the kicked-in gate and
        window, now shuttered tightly.

11   INT. GRANDPA SPELT'S HOUSE - MORNING

        Grandpa Spelt is seated at his desk. The large painting has
        been returned to its place.

                       GRANDPA SPELT
                You must go to the cave and recover
                the treasure before the pirates
                steal it. You are the only living
                descendant and will receive the
                treasure when I die.

        Grandpa Spelt wheezes, stressed from the night's ordeal.

        JACK SPELT, young, rugged, listens attentively. He scratches
        his head.

                       JACK SPELT
                Without a map, I'm not going to get   ⋏
                very far.

                       GRANDPA SPELT
                Precisely my boy, which is why I'm
                giving you this.

        Grandpa Spelt reaches under his desk and brings out an MP3
        RECORDER.

        Jack Spelt rises and stares at the gadget.

                       JACK SPELT
                A digital music player? I've always
                wanted one of those. But.. how on
                earth is it going to help me get
                the treasure?

                                              (CONTINUED)

If all the colors in the list are used (it does happen!) the entire script is re-printed in blue. Any changes to this "double-blue" revision are printed in "double-pink" and the whole cycle of colors begins again.

Revision Colors

A new color revision is issued every time the locked script is changed. Instead of numbered revisions, such as "Revision 1.0," followed by "Revision 2.0," the first "White Revision" is followed by the "Blue Revision." The colors progress in this order:

- White
- Blue
- Pink
- Yellow
- Green
- Goldenrod

- Buff
- Salmon
- Cherry
- Tan
- Gray
- Ivory

Since revisions usually change a few pages at most, the pages with changes are printed in the color of the revision and inserted into scripts, which are kept in three-ring binders, until everyone is walking around with a rainbow-colored script.

See how this works? Following proper locked-script procedure prevents the necessity of printing a new script every time something changes.

Here's a step-by-step guide to locking a screenplay in Celtx, and creating a shooting script.

White Revision

At the top of the screen, click **Script > Revision Mode...** The **Revision Options** window will appear. Check **Lock Scenes.** Rename "**Revision 1**" to

"White Revision" followed by the date. *"White Revision - mm/dd/yyyy."* Finally, click the **Revision Color** drop-down menu and change **Blue** to **White.**

Click the **Type/Set** tab at the bottom of the screen to preview the results. The title page should have the revision name and date under the script title, and all the scenes and pages in your script should be numbered. That was pretty easy!

If you don't see scene numbers, click the **Format Options** button, and in the **Show scene numbers** drop-down menu, change **None** to **Left.**

Do a **Save As...** and save your locked Celtx file with the revision color and date in the filename.

Unfortunately, revisions are the Achilles heel of Celtx. As of this writing, Celtx lacks the ability to:

1 Properly label revised pages with the revision color. Celtx renames every page in the shooting script with the new revision color, instead of just the pages changed, as is typically done.

2 You cannot export only the pages changed by a revision. For example, if the Blue revision has changed three pages of the White revision, and you want to send your friends the three new Blue pages and a Blue title page to insert into their White scripts, Celtx will not export these individual pages. Currently, Celtx only exports PDFs of the entire script.

This said, there is a slightly wonky workaround to these two problems.

Blue Revision

The Revision Mode toolbar is located directly above the script in the main Celtx window. To create a new revision, click the little green plus icon on the left.

As when creating the White revision, rename *"Revision 1"* to *"Blue Revision"* followed by the date. *"Blue Revision - mm/dd/yyyy."* Finally, click the *Revision Color* drop-down menu and change *White* to *Blue.*

Make your changes to the script. <u>This is the Blue Revision.</u> Do a *Save As...* and create a new Celtx file with the draft color and date in the filename:

"MyGreatScreenplay_BLUE-01-23-2011.celtx"

This will ensure the Blue revision is saved, and the White revision is preserved as a separate file.

Exporting Blue Pages

Export the entire Blue revision as a PDF, with the draft color and date in the PDF's filename:

"MyGreatScreenplay_BLUE-01-23-2011.pdf"

Using a PDF reader's *Print Range* feature (Adobe Reader, or equivalent) print only the title page and the pages changed in the blue revision, make copies with colored paper and a photocopier, and insert the pages into White revision scripts. Ta-da! Blue revision scripts!

Alternatively, you can print the Blue pages (on white paper) scan them into a PDF, and email them to your fellow animators, allowing them to print their own copies.

The absence of a proper revisions feature in Celtx can be a huge hassle, (especially when you start approaching the Cherry revision) but if you are working by yourself, or with a few additional people, revisions aren't as critical as they become on larger projects. If you're a serious filmmaker and thinking about writing your first feature film, or starting a project with a crew larger than five people, switch to commercial software such as Final Draft.

Storyboarding

Instead of writing a script, it is possible to draw an entire film in storyboard format and use it to make your film (though directors typically base their storyboards on a script they or someone else has written). If you can't be troubled to scribble out a script, at least take time to storyboard your film.

Storyboards are a lot like comic strips. Blank storyboards are sheets of paper covered with little squares. The movie is drawn into the squares shot by shot. Usually a few lines are written under the square describing what happens in the shot.

The storyboard helps you plan camera angles, character movement, set design, character design, prop placement, camera movement – all the visual elements of your film.

Storyboards also help you to visualize your movie before animating. This will assist you in cutting out unnecessary visuals that make movies slow and boring, instead of quick and snappy.

You may be thinking: *"I can't draw, so I can't make a storyboard."* If you can draw a stick figure with a nose, you can make a storyboard. Use the noses to show which way a figure is facing. That's it!

Robin Hood Storyboard

 Project **Robin Hood**  Scene **1, 2**

Robin Hood walks on the river-
bank

Little John walks on the river-
bank in Robin Hood's direction

Little John faces Robinhood

They fight!

Robin falls in the water

Little John laughs. Robin climbs
out of the river.

If you're drawing a storyboard from a script, each square in the storyboard should be labeled with the scene number, and a second number, the "shot number." The first storyboard square of the scene is **shot 1**, the second square is **shot 2**, and so on, as pictured here. If two squares are used to illustrate the same shot, they should be lettered. For example: "**1-2A**" and "**1-2B**".

Screenwriting Software

Final Draft. Many options for formatting and viewing your screenplay. Currently priced around $250.

Movie Magic Screenwriter. Comes with several templates and screenplay examples. Priced comparatively to Final Draft, about $250. Company has been noted for great customer service. Academic pricing is available for both Final Draft and Movie Magic.

www.finaldraft.com

www.screenplay.com

Celtx is an open-source program that contains many features of the programs above. The creators have moved away from their original business model and started charging for their software, but you can still download the open source version from our website and elsewhere.

www.celtx.com

www.stopmotionexplosion.com/downloads

WriterDuet and **Plotbot.** Online screenwriting tools are fabulous if you are working on a project with several people, and all of them need to access the script at once. The paid version of Celtx also has collaborative screenwriting features.

www.writerduet.com

www.plotbot.com

Chapter 4

Building Sets

 ets are the world your characters inhabit as they move through the events in your story. Stopmotion sets can be very simple. The story may take place on arctic ice, which could be made from a white tabletop and blue paper sky. Or the story could take place in a dusty western town, made of tan construction paper, storefronts constructed from LEGO® bricks, and distant mountains made from torn poster board.

Building Materials

Here's a bunch of stuff that could be used in a set. Acquire a new eye for everyday objects. Think: "What would this look like if I was three inches tall?"

Towel

Green: Grass, distant mountain, fuzzy slime monster.

Blue: Gigantic tidal wave, bottom of mysterious ocean cave, deep shag carpet.

Rug

Grab pillows, blocks, books and other bulky objects. Shove under rug to create instant hilly terrain.

Paper

Crumpled paper: Bush, tree, iceberg, boulder, termite mound, giant meteor.

Flat paper: Ground, sky, distant horizon, ice, water, road sign.

Cardboard box

Buildings, skyscrapers, apartments, shack, spaceship, boat, cliff walls. Dress up with more cardboard, make drawings, cut holes in the sides with a serrated knife, think of the box as a "base" to bulk up with other materials.

Packaging Stuff

Found in the boxes of new printers and computers. Ancient temple walls. The surface of a futuristic spacecraft. A hydroelectric dam.

Wire

Jungle vines, plumbing, iron rebar, rope.

Drinking straw

Steam pipes, flying saucer legs, smokestack, bazooka.

Ball of clay

Beanbag chair, TV set, fire hydrant, giant sunflower... Mold it into anything you want!

Additionally, you can animate inside the playsets created for some action figures. Nearly any construction themed toy can be used for set building. Use models from LEGO® sets, Playmobile® buildings, Lincoln Logs™, K'NEX® and so on.

If you wish to build more complex sets, research diorama modeling, model railway construction, doll house interior design and similar topics. Some of the I SPY (Scholastic) books contain great examples of worlds constructed in miniature.

Designing Sets

Before you start building, pull out your storyboards and study them. Look at all the different locations your characters visit, and the camera angles you have planned for each shot. When you finish you'll know the number of sets to build, and how they should be designed.

The process of reading a script and listing elements contained in it is called "breaking down" the script. If you followed the instructions above, you have created a "location breakdown."

If you listed all the props in the script, you would have a "prop breakdown." A list of all the vehicles would be called a "vehicle breakdown" and so on.

When designing the set, it's helpful to ask yourself three questions:

1 Where will the camera go?

2 Where will the lights go?

3 Where will my fingers go?

Indoor Sets

Interior sets can be built with one wall, two walls, or three. You'll want to leave at least one wall of the set open so the camera can see inside.

You can build sets with four walls, but make the walls easy to remove from the structure. If you need a different camera angle, you'll be able to pull the wall off the set and shoot from there.

The number of walls required depends on the camera angles you'll be using, and this can be quickly be determined by looking over your storyboards. (I told you storyboards were useful! If you haven't already, check them out on page 61) .

The walls should be tall enough so you can't see behind the set.

This set was used in the film *Jack Spelt and the Sandstone Caves*. The interior shots showed only the door, and the corner of the room, so just two walls had to be built, leaving the rest of the set open for animating work.

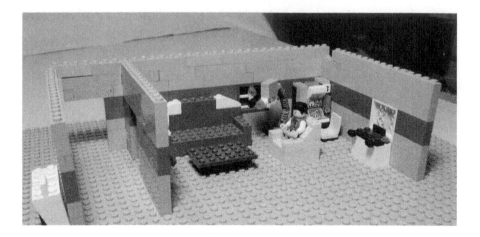

In the second set, I had shots of characters sitting on both sides of the room, so I built a set with three walls, and a hallway on the side.

Notice these sets do not have ceilings. Stopmotion sets with ceilings are a bad idea, since lighting is typically placed above the set, and ceilings make it harder to move your characters and props while you animate.

If you can see through windows in your set, create sky by placing some blue paper outside the window. You can create backdrops that look like buildings and animate cars driving by. Doing so enhances the illusion

that your set is located in a "real" world, surrounded by a dynamic, changing environment!

Outdoor Sets

It's important to have a nice backdrop. A big piece of sky-blue paper placed behind the set is a great starting place. It's easy to cut a few hills out of green paper, or the outlines of a few buildings, and tape them to the "sky." Some office and art supply stores sell sheets of poster board with printed clouds.

Green poster board is an excellent "grass" surface. You can also use green LEGO® baseplates, fabric, and other materials.

Another useful set-building material is a foamcore folding panel that's typically used for displays at science fairs. It stands up by itself, and can surround a small set.

If you have certain kinds of action, like a car on the road or a flying plane, you can keep the object in one place and move the background instead of the car. This is technique is similar to the "looping backgrounds" seen in some cartoons.

City Sets

The simplest way to make buildings for your stop motion city? Build false fronts with nothing behind them. If you construct a bunch of these fake buildings and set them up in a row, they look great!

If your building materials are limited, pull out your storyboards and set breakdown. Pick out all the shots that take place on one set. Build the set, capture all the shots, then pull the set apart and build it into

something new. If you're creating a LEGO® movie with a small collection of bricks, you can reuse them over and over again. It's time-consuming to move back and forth between two sets. When possible, animate all the footage of a set in one go, then move to the next set.

Securing Your Sets

Imagine you're animating an exciting part of your movie:

Flying Fennris, pro skateboarder, is burning up the pavement. He swerves around a light pole. He grinds down a handrail. Suddenly the ground starts shaking back and forth. Fennris isn't fazed. He tears up the street like gravity is out of style. Despite his entire world moving every few frames, he doesn't feel it!

If this describes your animating experience, you probably forgot to fasten your set to the table. Adjusting a character or object between frames is enough to nudge the set out of alignment. Also, don't rule out the possibility of bumps and knocks from your own elbows and sleeves!

Stick the set to your table with double sided tape, or hold it down with c-clamps and heavy books.

Ooops... Someone forgot the tape!

This animation setup is a simple plywood table built into a corner of a closet.
The wire shelf above the set is convenient for storing supplies and hanging lights.

Another way to lessen noticeable bumps is to attach your camera to the set itself. When you move your set accidentally, the camera moves with the set and the movement isn't as noticeable. You'll need a large base for the set, and you'll still need to be sure the lighting stays in the right places.

Chapter 5

Cameras

To create stopmotion films, you'll need a camera that sends a video image to your computer. If you're a beginner, you'll want a camera that is small, easy to use, and inexpensive.

All of these qualities are found in a webcam, a small camera typically used for video chatting over the Internet. Webcams offer the most bang for the animator's buck!

You can also use camcorders and digital still cameras for animating. If you are looking for the best possible image quality, use a digital camcorder, or digital still camera. These cameras are introduced at the end of this chapter.

Choosing a Camera

The price of high-quality webcams continues to drop, but manufacturers are accomplishing this by discarding features necessary for creating animations. There are several features you'll want to look for.

- **Manual controls**. Many cheaper cameras have "fixed focus" and automatically adjust the image settings when the camera's environment changes. Automatic controls are great if you're using a webcam to chat with friends or film a video blog post, but they can cause problems for animators. Before buying a camera, check to see which controls you can set manually. Make sure it's possible to adjust the camera's focus, exposure, and white balance manually.

- **Macro Focus**. You should be able to focus on objects that are very close to the camera lens – 1½ inches (3 cm) if possible.

- **Image Resolution**. The bigger your camera sensor is, the sharper and clearer the image created will be. It's common to find 1.3 **MP** (**megapixel**) webcams, which capture standard definition footage. A 2.1 MP camera captures HD video.

- Some webcams have a small clip or "hinge" which is used to attach the camera to various surfaces. Make sure you can still set the camera on a flat surface, without it tipping over.

It's common to find small cameras embedded in laptops and some new desktops. These cameras can be used for animating, if you're animating larger subjects, like a drawing on a whiteboard, people, stuffed animals, etc.

Some cameras also have a threaded hole, allowing the camera to be mounted on a tripod. This is a nice extra.

Mac and Windows Webcams

In the past, webcams had the most support on Windows-based computers. This changed as Macs increased in popularity.

Now, pretty much all webcams have plug-and-play support on OS X. Webcams that conform to the **UVC (USB Video Class)** are compatible with OS X 10.4.3 and all later versions, as well as all versions of Windows, from XP to the present.

If you are using an old version of OS X, the **Macam** community may have a driver that is compatible with your webcam. If your camera is supported and on the list, you can download and install a free OS X driver.

Camera Words

Pixel: The camera sensor converts an image into thousands of tiny colored dots, called pixels.

Sensor: An electronic chip that converts light into numbers, telling the computer the brightness and color that a picture contains. There are two types of sensors: CCD and CMOS. A webcam sensor might have "300K" pixels, meaning 300,000. A digital still camera might have "3 Megapixels," or 3 million pixels.

CCD: A type of sensor used in some webcams. These are hard to find. Typically, they are more expensive.

CMOS: A type of sensor used in most newer webcams.

Resolution: The number of pixels an image contains. The more pixels a picture has, the better quality it will be. A 720 x 1280 image is 1280 pixels wide and 720 tall (a good resolution for simple stopmotion work).

Auto Exposure: Most webcams have software that automatically adjusts the exposure to keep the picture well lit. When you're animating, you'll want to turn off this feature and set the exposure yourself.

While most cameras come with Windows drivers and software, you may have to visit the manufacturer's website for a Mac driver, or use a driver created by a third party. If this is not available, check out the **Webcam Settings** app, available in the App Store. This program provides some level of control for most webcams on OS X.

Stopmotion Explosion Webcams

While companies such as Logitech, Microsoft and Creative continue to manufacture high-quality webcams, the features of these cameras have become increasingly geared towards video-chatting, with few manual controls.

If you visit the Stopmotion Explosion website, you'll find two HD-capable cameras with manual features suitable for animators.

A shiny Stopmotion Explosion 1080p Widescreen Video Webcam! Manual focus, image controls and 1920 x 1080 resolution video. Get 'em while they last.

Camera Image Controls

You will encounter these controls in the menus of nearly any camera you use. Don't be afraid to grab knobs and sliders and tweak them until you understand what they do. This is a camera, not the control room of a nuclear power plant!

Brightness: The eye's perception of light in an image. Cameras that let you control brightness do so by adding light to all the colors in the image.

Contrast: The eye's perception of difference in brightness or color between details of a picture that are next to each other. Adjusting contrast takes light away from dimmer areas and adds more light to the brighter areas of a picture.

Gain: An electronic enhancement that affects brightness. Increasing the gain makes dimly lit areas seem brighter without changing the exposure. This can produce "noise" or graininess in the picture.

Gamma: Refers to an electronic correction that is used to keep colors looking natural on different media such as computer monitors, photo prints, and color printers.

Hue: Changes the way the camera "sees" color. If you want to adjust the color of your image, you're better off adjusting the white balance.

Saturation: Controls the amount of color in an image. A highly saturated image has lots of color. Low saturation produces a black-and-white image.

Exposure: The amount of time the camera allows light to fall on the electronic sensor. The higher the exposure level is set, the brighter the picture will be—but if set too high, the picture will look washed out. Also called "shutter speed."

Flicker: Settings compensate for flicker created by fluorescent lighting. Cameras are sensitive to this. In the US use the "60Hz" setting.

White Balance: Adds color to the image until white objects appear white. In the camera, ordinary light bulbs will appear "warmer" and reddish, while fluorescents and sunlight will appear "cooler" and blue.

Using a Webcam

As soon as you get your webcam out of its packaging, follow the manufacturer's installation instructions.

To test the camera, start up your framegrabber software.

A live picture should appear in the software's video window. If the image is blurry, twist the

A webcam plugged into a computer's USB port

focus ring encircling the lens until the picture is clear.

If your camera doesn't have manual focus (a focus ring), you can still use the camera for basic animation purposes, but it's fairly useless. You won't be able to capture the close up images that really bring stopmotion to life.

Your camera is set up and ready to use. If you have enough light and the picture looks decent, you could move onto the next chapter and try a little animating. If you want to keep tweaking the camera settings for the best image possible, read the next section.

Camera Controls

Taking time to master your camera's controls will improve the image quality of your productions.

Your stopmotion software should have an option on the menu called *Camera Controls*, *Camera Options, Source* or something similar.

This screenshot shows where to find the camera settings in **Stopmotion Explosion Animator** (SME).

Laptops with internal webcams are becoming commonplace, which means you'll have multiple cameras attached to the computer. In these situations you'll need to select the camera you're using in the animation software. In SME, click **Options > Camera Source...**

The camera menu pictured may differ from the menu for your camera, but you'll find the same basic image controls in the software for most web cameras.

Have your set well lit and the webcam in place before starting these adjustments.

Exposure

In SME, click *Options* then *Capture Controls*. Depending on the camera you're using, you will see a window with several tabs. In the *Camera Control*, or *Settings* tab, uncheck the *Auto* box next to the *Exposure* slider. Adjusting the camera's exposure changes the brightness of the image. If the exposure is allowed to automatically adjust itself, flickers and changes in image brightness may appear. For example, if your hand reaches into the set to move something, the automatic exposure will kick in, and the camera image will become brighter. The adjustment takes a few seconds. If you grab a frame before the picture returns to its original state, this brighter frame will be visible in the completed footage, creating an unwanted flicker.

After turning off automatic exposure, you will need to set the exposure to a desirable level. Move the exposure slider until the picture is bright again.

White Balance

White balance allows you to compensate for different colors of light by changing the color of white in an image.

Confused? Let me explain. If you're inside reading this book next to a lamp, the light shining on the pages is yellow. The camera sees the yellowish light and adjusts colors until the lamp light shining on the page appears pure white.

White balance is set by placing the camera in front of a white object, like a piece of paper, and pushing or clicking a button that "sets" the balance. The camera tweaks the image until the paper is white.

To manually set the white balance on your camera, uncheck the auto box. Place a sheet of white paper in front of the camera. Check the auto box again. The camera will sample the white of the paper and adjust accordingly. If you continue animating with the same lighting, you won't have to set the white balance again.

Other Settings

Some cameras have the ability to adjust for flicker created by fluorescent lights. If your camera has an anti-flicker control, try setting it to 50 or 60Hz.

Other settings, like brightness and contrast, are fairly self-explanatory. Take a few moments to play with the sliders and watch their effect on the image.

In addition to the image controls mentioned here, some cameras have an autofocus setting. This is found in digital video cameras, and some higher-end webcams. If possible, turn the autofocus control off, and adjust the focus manually.

Using Camcorders

If you own a camcorder, you have access to some nice features.

- Real optical zoom, not a "fake" digital zoom, which is simply the camera doubling the size of the image and discarding the edges of the frame, making everything seem closer.

- Greater image control, more settings to tweak, and better low-light performance.

All this production-enhancing goodness could be featured in your next film if you had a way to connect the camera to your computer. How do you do this?

Digital Camcorders

Digital camcorders output video through FireWire connectors.

This is what a FireWire port on the computer looks like. Sometimes you'll see the number "1394," sometimes you'll see a FireWire symbol. These ports come in 6 and 4-pin versions.

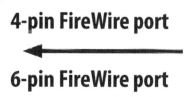

4-pin FireWire port

6-pin FireWire port

This is what a FireWire cable looks like. Notice the large and small ends. Typically, the larger 6-pin connector plugs into the computer and the small 4-pin connector plugs into the camera.

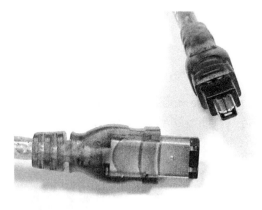

It's common for laptop computers to have a small 4-pin FireWire port instead of the larger 6-pin style. You can purchase adapters that will convert a large 6-pin FireWire cable into the smaller four-pin version. These are very handy.

Once the computer and camera are connected, you can use the camcorder like an ordinary webcam.

By using your camera's zoom, you should be able to get good closeups even if the camera is too big to fit into your set.

Camcorder Driver

In some instances, a special driver is required to use camcorders with animation programs. This driver can be downloaded from:

stopmotionexplosion.com/downloads

Whether you're using an analog or digital camera, you'll need to make all adjustments and changes to the camera controls through the camera's menus, buttons and switches.

Many camcorders have an autofocus setting that should be disabled, otherwise the camera will constantly be focusing on your fingers as you move them in and out of the set. Auto exposure should also be disabled.

Use your camera's AC adapter and plug into a power outlet, otherwise you'll run out of battery power long before your animating session is over.

Digital Still Cameras

Stopmotion does not necessarily require a camera that's capable of capturing video. You're capturing one frame at a time, so still cameras can be used.

A digital still camera, capturing images with millions of pixels offers the ultimate in video resolution, which is why they are the camera of choice for high-end stopmotion films.

In-Camera Animation

Many people are already using a digital still camera to animate. They take pictures of their characters moving, one picture at a time, and "play" the pictures by quickly scrolling through them with the camera's preview button. This is a simple way to make animations with a point-'n-shoot camera, or DSLR, but you can do better!

Camera Problems

Most stopmotion software functions by grabbing frames from a live video source. This presents a problem because most digital cameras will not send video to the computer, even when the two are connected by a USB cable.

If you want to try extracting video from a digital camera, you're more likely to find VIDEO OUT through RCA jacks or HDMI cables. Some cameras have this feature, so check the camera's manual. Again, you won't be getting the camera's full resolution, so this is like using a still camera as a low-resolution webcam.

Many DSLRs, such as those sold by Nikon and Canon have a feature called Live View, which allows the camera the camera to be controlled via USB. You can purchase stopmotion programs that take advantage of this functionality, and do some basic animation with the manufacturer's camera control software. This is further discussed in the **Animating with DSLRs** chapter.

You can still use a digital camera for stopmotion, even if it doesn't have Live View. Here's one way to accomplish this.

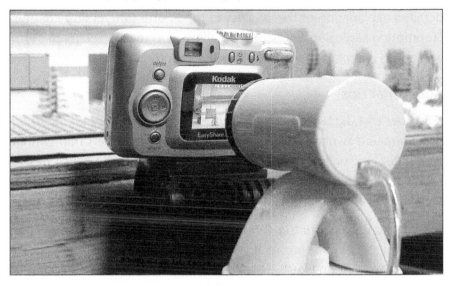

Here, a webcam is pointing at the camera's little preview screen. The webcam is plugged into a computer running SME, or your favorite stopmotion framegrabber.

Every time you take a picture with the still camera, you grab a frame in the framegrabber. This creates a low-resolution preview of your work, which can be played back for reference. You can discard the preview when you're done. The real frames of the animation remain on the camera's memory card.

Make sure the camera is fastened down tightly while snapping frames (if your camera can use a remote shutter release, go ahead and purchase one. You want to touch the camera little as possible).

Frame Conversion

When you're finished animating with your still camera, you've created hundreds and hundreds of picture files that need to be converted into a single video file, or several video files, depending on the number of scenes you're animated.

It's fairly easy to convert a series of pictures into video. You'll find a detailed explanation of the process in the **Frame Conversion** chapter. Stopmotion Explosion Animator also allows you to convert images into video. This is explained in the **Animating** chapter.

Additional Tips

Most low-end digital still cameras suffer from a flicker problem. When the animation is played back, you see a flicker between frames that are lighter and darker than others. The lens is often the cause of this problem, and there's not much you can do about it. The cause, and a solution is presented in the **Animating with DSLRs** chapter.

A final warning. Capturing thousands and thousands of frames may damage your camera shutter. If your camera is important to you, don't risk it on stopmotion films!

Using & Improving Webcams

Webcams come in many shapes and sizes. Nearly every design has a few weaknesses – weaknesses that can be mended with strategic application

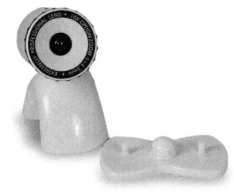

of high-tech materials (typically tape and rubber bands).

I prefer smaller tube-shaped cameras because they are easier to fit into tiny animation sets. You can however use any camera, regardless of shape.

Let's take a look at a random tube-shaped webcam, and figure out how it could be improved for animating.

This particular webcam has a detachable plate on the bottom with a threaded hole that fits a standard tripod screw. Other cameras may have a clamp, or clip for attaching to surfaces.

The ring around the lens is the *focus ring*. Sometimes this is a little wheel on the camera body. Sometimes the lens itself is twisted to adjust focus. In some higher-end cameras, particularly those with automatic focus, the camera dialog box on the computer has controls for changing the focus. When you have a manual focus ring, twisting it to the left focuses on far-away things. Twist it right to focus on close-up objects.

Focus

Many webcams have a button on top that lets you grab single frames and save them to your computer. Making animations this way is <u>not</u> recommended, unless the camera is *extremely* stable. Otherwise the image will jump every time you push the button.

This camera is connected to the stand with a swivel joint. While swivel joints are handy for positioning the camera, they're usually at fault when the camera gets joggled. Just wiggling the cord often swivels the camera off target.

One way to fix this problem is by wrapping a rubber band tightly between the camera and stand. Your goal is to immobilize this

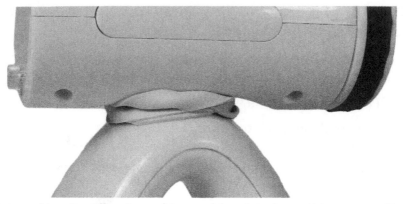

joint, making it stiffer. (I used two rubber bands on this camera. You'll need more if yours aren't very thick).

Done! Grab some tape for the next step.

I used black electrical tape, because it's sticky, easy to cut, and doesn't leave a residue on the camera. Also, black tape *just looks cool*, but any tape should work fine.

If you want to keep the camera's swivel feature, this step should be skipped. If you continue wrapping, you'll lose the

ability to swivel the camera back and forth, but the camera will have maximum stability.

Check out some of the other camera stability ideas here.

When using the Stopmotion Explosion 1080P camera, I like to tape one end down to the table.

This Stopmotion Explosion 720p Webcam has been clamped to a stack of LEGO® bricks. Fastening the camera to a set is easy!

Here is another LEGO® webcam stand, this one using a round camera.

CHECK IT OUT!

Links

Macam:

webcam-osx.sourceforge.net

Chapter 6

Lighting

 ilmmaking has been called "painting with light". Good lighting is key to creating a visually dynamic picture.

Bad Lights

A couple of light sources should be avoided.

- **Ceiling Lights**: Light fixtures on the ceiling aren't bright enough, and light falling over your shoulder onto the set will create shadows. You need to bring the light *to* your set.

- **The Sun:** The sun moves, and clouds keep passing overhead, creating shadows. Animating outdoors would require working quickly, on a perfect day. Since these two factors are tough to control, it's better to find other light sources.

Good Lights

A few desk lamps, clip lights, or a mix of both can provide plenty of light. Lights are especially useful if they have clamps or clips of some kind, allowing them to be placed creatively during setup, and secured tightly during filming.

Preferably, your animation setup should be lit with two or three lights, set up in a way that corresponds roughly to the rules of three-point lighting.

Three Point Lighting

Using the basic "three-point" lighting technique, lights are placed on the left and right sides of a subject. A third light is directed at the subject from behind. If you're lighting a person, this creates a edge of light on the subject's shoulders and hair, helping to separate them from the background. A fourth light (if needed) is used to light the background.

Three-Point Lighting

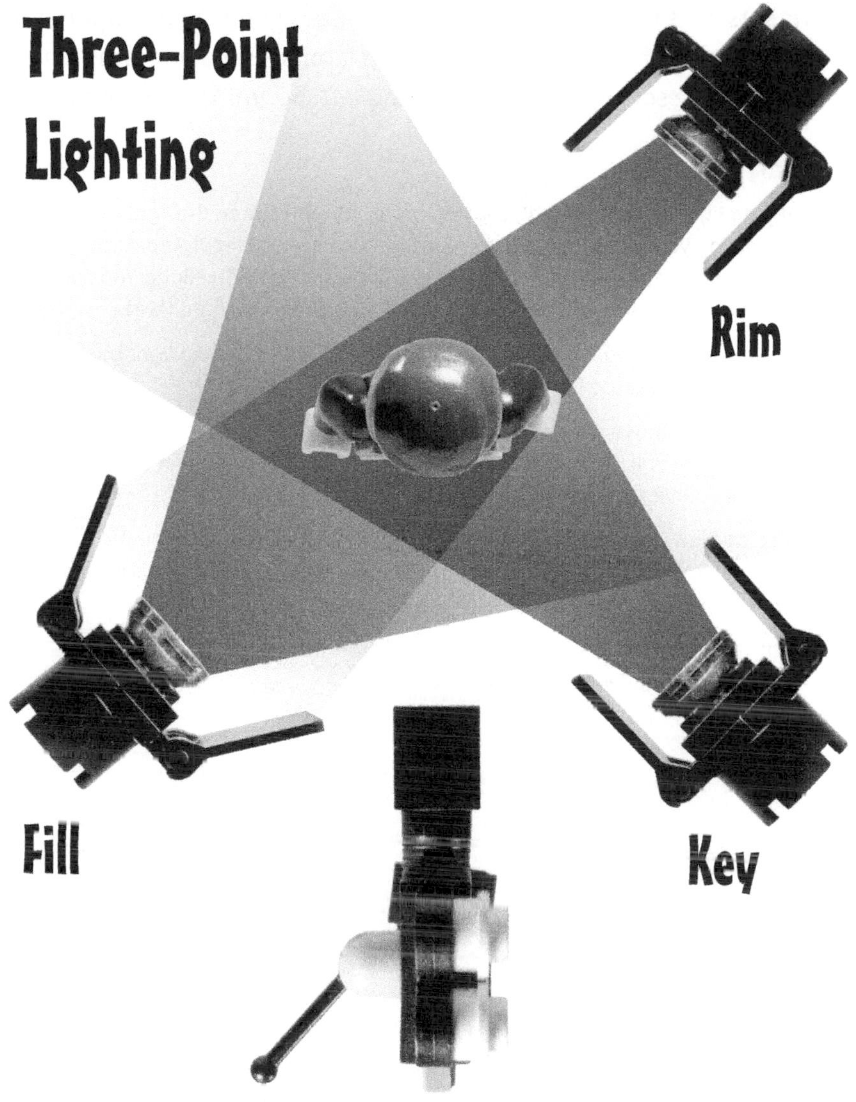

Rim

Fill

Key

*A bright focused light is placed on one side of the subject. This light is called the **Key**. The **Fill**, a smaller light is placed on the opposite side, filling in shadows created by the Key. A Fill light doesn't have to be pointed directly at the subject, it can be bounced off walls and flat, light-colored surfaces. The **Rim** light is pointed at the subject from behind, separating the subject from the background.*

If your sets and figures are small, you can easily light your animation setup with two light sources (say two desk lamps). Place one lamp on the right side of the set, and the other on the left. Boom! You're done.

Lighting Tweaks

- If your lighting is too bright, causing glare, you can soften the light by bouncing your light sources off the walls and other light-colored surfaces, like white poster board. This will diffuse and spread out the light. You can also purchase and use a dimmer switch for greater control of light levels.

- Wear dark clothing. Light colors, like white and yellow, reflect light back on the set, which can cause flicker problems

- Block out as much natural light as possible and avoid light sources placed behind you. Pull down all the shades and shut off every lamp in the room except your set lights.

- Use caution when animating with desk lamps! Use bulbs with the recommended wattage, and be careful... they can get hot! Turn your lights off when you leave the room.

- The lamps pictured here use LED bulbs. LED lights use less electricity, and stay cooler than regular light bulbs.

This simple scoop light fixture can be purchased from Lowes.
It attaches to pretty much anything.

Check out this super-awesome basement animation table! It's made so you can stand up while animating. The animation table is stacked on top of a folding table for extra height. LED lights are clipped to the floor joists and backgrounds can be attached to the wall.

Lighting & Camera Settings

Does the video you create flicker, even though you've carefully controlled the lighting? The camera's auto exposure setting may be turned on. Auto exposure monitors the light falling on the camera's sensor. If the light changes – for example, if your hand moves in front of the camera for a moment, auto exposure compensates by changing the camera settings.

Your stopmotion software may have an option in one menu labeled *Camera controls*, *Camera options* or something similar. It will display a window with several controls that modify the camera's image, the color, brightness, saturation, exposure, and so on.

If *Exposure* is set to *Auto*, uncheck the box, or check *Manual. Exposure Lock* might be another label for this setting.

If you are animating with a camcorder attached to the animation software, you will have to change this setting in the camera menus. Consult your camera's instruction book.

Now, when you put your hand in front of the camera, the lighting won't be affected. When you take your hand away, the picture will remain the same.

Image Banding

For my light setup, I've started using LED bulbs in combination with a dimmer switch. The dimmer makes it easy to crank the light up, or bring it down as needed. It also gives me a way to solve image banding issues.

Image banding is occasionally encountered when using LED lights, or compact fluorescent lights (CFLs).

Image banding looks like a row of gray lines across your video image

Whether or not you'll have a problem with banding depends on the bulb you're using. In my experience, I've seen banding occur with daylight temperature (5500k) LED lights, but not had a problem with indoor temperature (3200k) lights.

To fix banding, I crank up the camera exposure, making the camera more sensitive to light, then bring down the LED light brightness with my dimmer switch. This makes the banding go away.

Dimmer switch. A tiny device that solves a world of problems!

Lighting Effects

Flashlights are handy for mood lighting. Think of them as little spotlights. If your flashlight is bright and focused, it will create a small spot of glare in the camera's image.

This glare can be an explosion, arc-welding flare, rocket lift-off, transporter beam, or whatever the story needs. Enhance the effect by moving the flashlight slightly in each frame.

By wrapping colored plastic wrap or tissue paper over a flashlight, the light can be red, orange, yellow (good fire colors), or green and blue (space, night effects).

This cool effect was created with a few cotton balls and a flashlight, which is hiding behind the cotton at the center of the explosion. For more explosion effects, turn to page 162.

Using Laser Pointers

Kids, ask permission before using one of these. Never look directly at a laser pointer's beam!

Fire

Scraps of colored plastic, or small transparent red, yellow and orange LEGO® bricks are a great fire "base." Use a flashlight pointing down on the flames for some glow.

The red dot of a laser pointer looks "grainy" when you capture it with a webcam. These grains (or dots) can achieve the illusion of leaping flames. If you shine the pointer at a transparent plastic object, it creates a glowing light effect. Laser "fires"

Bandits around the campfire

look best with very little extra lighting. The laser beam will wash out in a brightly lit scene.

Indoor Lighting

Putting a flashlight inside a house set is a quick way to create a warm glow inside.

You can enhance the glow by taping paper, or small pieces of masking tape across the inside of the windows. These coverings will catch and diffuse the light, making it easier to see.

Ever look outside your window and see pirates in the yard?

Lightning

This is an easy, fun effect to create!

1. Turn off all your set lights except one. Move it back far enough so the set is fairly dark.

2. Start rapidly clicking the capture button.

3. Quickly swing the light towards the set, and away from the set. You'll see the frames of your animation brighten and darken.

4. When editing the film, add thunderclap sound effects.

By swinging a light source around and capturing frames, you can create lightning effects like this!

Chapter 7

Composition

Starry Night by Vincent van Gogh.

 omposition is the art of arranging elements within a picture in such a way that the image is balanced and pleasing to the eye.

If you look at a picture and squint, the tiny details disappear, and you see a collection of lines, shapes, and colors. The arrangement of these elements pull the eye towards certain areas, and away from others.

103

Composition is an important storytelling tool. Filmmakers want the audience to notice specific details during the progression of their film, and composition is a means by which this is accomplished.

Here's an example. A showdown between the town bully and a little cowpoke. To emphasize the large, imposing bully, we film him from below.

Mesquite Mike does not like Panhandle Pete.

To emphasize the insignificance of the cowpoke, we film him from an upper angle, as if we were the bully looking down on the brim of his hat.

Panhandle Pete is surprised to see Mesquite Mike.

As you plan the composition of your shots, choose angles that tell the story of your movie.

Rule of Thirds

Dividing an image into halves should be avoided. This is called "bisecting." Nature is rarely bisected. Instead we find collections of objects clumped into harmonious balance. We can avoid bisecting by applying the **Rule of Thirds.**

To apply this rule, mentally divide your image into a perfect tic-tac-toe grid with four intersecting lines. Place areas of interest so they fall under or around the four points.

Look at the image of a man and his motorcycle. The character is underneath the left line with his face almost beneath the top left cross. The motorcycle is underneath the lower right cross and bottom horizontal line.

Rule of Thirds grid. Important areas fall where the lines cross.

As a rule of thumb, keep important things out of the middle of the squares and under the lines. This will ensure your shot is composed correctly.

Lines and Triangles

When framing and composing your shots, always remember "less is more." The most brilliant compositions are not the most cluttered, but those that draw attention to essential areas, and tell a story with them.

Triangle Rule

Important objects in an image should be arranged in such a way that they form a triangle. The viewer follows the lines of this triangle, until the eye has visited every area of the image.

In this picture, you can see how a triangle is formed by the character's face, the door of the house, and the motorcycle wheel.

Lines of Composition

Lines in your image also form triangles, which emphasize certain areas.

See how the lines created by the top and bottom of the house point towards the character's face? Additional lines along the bottom of the image point towards the motorcycle. Finally, the character forms a triangle, which again draws the eye towards his face.

Composition can be learned by studying art and images around you. As an exercise, try tracing triangles of composition in a magazine or newspaper ad.

Frames and Composition

You may have heard of "widescreen" and "standard" video. These terms refer to the shape of the video frame. The shape of the frame will change the image's composition.

4:3 Frame

16:9 Frame

An "aspect ratio" is two numbers, the ratio of the long side of a shape to the short side of a shape.

For example, the aspect ratio of a 4-by-3 rectangle is 4:3. This is the aspect ratio of a standard definition video frame.

Widescreen video has an aspect ratio of 16:9. All HD cameras shoot widescreen video.

The flat rectangular shape of a widescreen frame offers more creative composition possibilities than the square 4:3 frame. Also, human eyes see the world in widescreen, so this frame looks most natural to us.

The composition of the 4:3 image here is so-so. Key elements are placed under the thirds grid, but there's a lot of blank space at the top and bottom of the frame.

After the frame is cropped to the bottom 16:9 image, the thirds grid has changed, and the composition looks a lot better.

The rules of composition can be broken for storytelling effect. If a filmmaker wanted to capture the essence of a tiny, claustrophobic space, they could use tight, badly composed angles. Good filmmakers understand and apply rules of composition, but they know when to break the rules.

Selective Focus

Hold your finger close to your eye and look at it. Notice how everything behind your finger blurs out? Achieving this effect with a camera is called selective focus, or **Depth of Field (DOF)**. If an image has "deep" DOF, everything in the image will appear sharply in focus. If an image has "shallow" DOF, a small part of the image will be in focus.

Shallow DOF allows the camera and audience to focus on specific areas of an scene. Deep DOF shows all areas of the image at once.

Focus on the foreground character

In these two images, you can see how shallow DOF allows you to selectively draw attention to characters in the foreground and background.

Although webcams and consumer grade camcorders do not allow you to control the depth of field, this is possible if you use a lens with an aperture ring. Turn to the **Animating with DSLRs** chapter for more information on this topic.

Focus on the background character

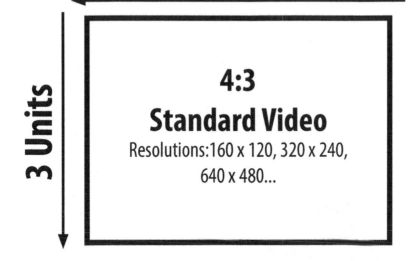

4 Units

3 Units

4:3
Standard Video
Resolutions:160 x 120, 320 x 240,
640 x 480...

16 Units

9 Units

16:9
Widescreen Video
Resolutions:640 x 360, 852 x 480,
1280 x 720, 1920 x 1080...

HEY!
Download these
animation programs
for FREE
StopmotionExplosion.com/
downloads

Chapter 8

Animating

You have a story, a set, some lights, a camera and it's time to call ACTION! Learn basic animation skills with Stopmotion Explosion Animator, the software we've created to make animation fun and easy for everyone.

Animation Techniques

Before digging into the stopmotion software, let's take a look at some commonly animated movements.

Walking and Running

The movements of the walk cycle and run cycle are important to master, because most movies feature characters walking or running around.

Here is a series of pictures showing the exact movements of a walk cycle using a LEGO® minifig. (These little plastic people are great to practice with).

Walk Cycle

- The figure's arms swing, but only a little.
- The left arm goes forward with the right foot, and vice versa.
- After the last frame of the sequence above, the figure repeats the cycle, this time leading with the left foot.
- Focus on keeping the minifig's torso upright. Leaning too far forward is a common mistake beginners make.

Run Cycle

- The character's arms swing more.
- He leans forward a bit more.
- He covers more ground with each step.
- After the last frame, the cycle begins on the opposite foot.

Think. How do you walk? What movements are made? Watch someone walking. How could you break the movements down into minifig size?

How Fast? Frames Per Second (FPS)

Your animation software will have a way to set the "frame rate," "fps" or "frames per second." This is the number of frames that fill one second of film. The higher your frame rate is, the smoother your animation will appear. However, you'll have to capture all those frames, so animating will take longer.

Minifig Walk Cycle

A LEGO® minifig walking at 15 frames per second.

Stikfa Walk Cycle

A stikfa walking at 15 frames per second. These movements can be used with ModiBots, or any complex two-legged figure.

A LEGO® minifig running at 15 FPS

Animators using 35mm film cameras animate at 12 or 24 fps, as film plays at 24 frames per second. To animate at 12 fps, they simply grab two frames at a time, halving the frame rate. Most simple animations use a frame rate of 10, 12 or 15 FPS.

Mouth Animation

Speech can be broken down into individual sounds. These sounds are called **Phonemes**. The chart in this chapter shows the shapes the human mouth forms when it sounds out a phoneme.

A character says the phrase:

"Lock the door tonight."

Video Tutorials: Walk & Run Cycles

stopmotionexplosion.com/walk-cycle

stopmotionexplosion.com/run-cycle

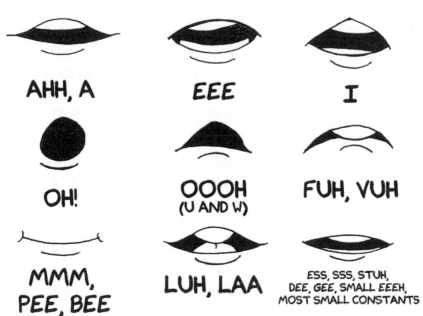

AHH, A   EEE   I

OH!   OOOH   FUH, VUH
       (U AND W)

MMM,   LUH, LAA   ESS, SSS, STUH,
PEE, BEE   DEE, GEE, SMALL EEEH,
                        MOST SMALL CONSTANTS

The *Luh, (Lock) Ess, (the) Ooh (door) Ess, Ess (tonight)* shapes would be used to animate this phrase (picture on page 115).

This isn't obvious from the text of the phrase. Try saying the phrase yourself in front of a mirror. Look at the shapes your own mouth makes.

The key to making great lip-animation is to focus on how words sound, rather than the letters themselves. Animate sound shapes, not letter shapes.

Mouth shapes do not have to be frame-perfect. The art of lip animation is more impressionistic than exact. The sounds of speech flow together, and the shapes do as well.

Anticipate the sound. Show the mouth shape slightly before the character vocalizes the sound itself.

Using a webcam to record and replay your own lip movements while speaking can take the guesswork out of breaking phrases down into individual shapes.

Lips

Adding animated lips to a character can be done in several ways. All lip-animation techniques require the character dialog to be recorded before animating, as the lip shapes and shape-timing is derived from the dialog. The method used depends on the kind of character being animated, and what "look" the animator is trying to achieve.

The animator can make several heads, model each head with a different phoneme shape, then swap heads as needed. If a soft material, like clay is being animated, the mouth shapes can be molded into the head. Alternatively, the animator can make just the mouth shapes, and swap out the mouth (this technique is used in the *Wallace and Gromit* films).

Mouth shapes can be added after animating, with a video-compositing program, such as **Adobe After Effects.** Using this technique, the characters are animated with blank heads. The mouth-shapes are drawn and composited onto the head after animating.

Stopmotion in 6 Steps

1 Sets, characters, and props are placed in front of the camera. The framegrabber (stopmotion software) is launched.

2 Clicking a button in the software "grabs" a frame from the camera.

3 The animator moves the characters a little bit, pulls their fingers out of the scene and grabs another frame from the camera.

4 This process continues until the animator has "grabbed" many frames.

5 The program plays the grabbed frames back, allowing the animator to preview the animation.

6 When the animation is finished the program assembles the frames into a movie file.

Let's apply these steps in a stopmotion film of our own!

Animation Software for Windows & OS X

In this book, you'll find instructions for **Stopmotion Explosion Animator** and **Stopmotion Explosion Animator for OS X.**

Lip shapes added to a character after animating using video compositing techniques

While the programs in this book can be downloaded from our site for free, advanced users may eventually outgrow their features, and wish to move to paid software. For OS X users wishing to upgrade, I recommend **iStopMotion**, and for Windows users, I recommend **Dragonframe**. Free trials are available for both programs.

Finally, users on old Windows computers may want to try the **Stop Motion Animator** application, which can be also be downloaded for free from the Stopmotion Explosion website. This application is optimized for slower systems.

Intro to Stopmotion Explosion Animator

Stopmotion Explosion Animator (SME) was created with the idea that animators want to be able to work with both individual frames of their animation and video files. This makes it easier to edit the animation frames with an image editor (as described in the **Flight** and **Art of War** chapters), without the intermediate step of converting a video file into images for editing.

If you're just beginning your animation adventure, this functionality may not make much sense, or seem important. Don't worry about it. For now, it's time to start learning basic animation skills with SME.

Assemble your set, gather your actors, place your lights, and plug in your camera. Start by clicking the icon on your desktop, or visiting the directory the program was installed in.

You should see a video image in the preview window. If you see an image from your computer's internal camera (many laptops ship with an internal camera for video chatting), select the correct camera by clicking *Options > Camera Source...* To increase the camera resolution, refer to the steps on page 126.

After adjusting the camera's focus, image brightness and color, and

(assuming the camera is pointed at something you want to animate) click the *Start* button in the upper left corner of the control window. This will open up a file dialog. Navigate to the directory where you wish to save files, and type in a name for your animation. Then click *Save.* Congratulations! You've captured the first frame of the animation.

Notice the *Start* button has changed to *Grab*. Click *Grab*, move your actors and props slightly, click *Grab* again, and repeat.

The frame-counter tells you how many frames you've shot. When you've shot a few seconds of video, around 30 or 40 frames,

Video Tutorial: SME Animator

To watch video tutorials that explain how to use Stopmotion Explosion Animator, visit: *stopmotionexplosion.com/sme*

click the *Play* button and watch the footage you've created. If you want to add more frames to the animation, continue with more movements and grabs. If you mess up, click *Delete* to remove frames. When your scene is complete, click *Make Movie*, export the file, and you've completed your first animated video!

You don't need to open SME to play the video after it's been saved to the disk. Just double-click the video file. Your computer's media player will launch and start playing what you created.

SME: Advanced Features

The frame rate is set to 15 frames per second by default. You may select other frame rates from the *"15 FPS"* drop-down menu.

To navigate through the animation one frame at a time, click and drag the timeline slider. You'll notice this changes the preview window from a live camera image, to an image of an animation frame. To switch back to the live camera image, click the *Live* button.

Clicking the *Live* button is also a useful way to compare the last frame in the animation to the frame you're about to capture.

If you have at least one frame in your animation, you can click the *Onion Skin* button to activate a special preview mode.

Onion Skinning

When you move a figure, it helps to see how the new position lines up to the last frame captured. Some animation programs give you a way to do this. This feature is called **onion skinning**.

121

Here's a visual demonstration of onion skinning. The top image shows the last frame captured.

In the second frame the character has bent forward slightly. With onion skinning turned on, the frame and the character's new position have been blended together in the camera window. It's easy to see how far the character has moved.

When the character is in the right place, a frame can be grabbed. You can continue grabbing frames, and previewing the character's position using onion skinning until the animation is complete.

Onion skinning is also handy when you've knocked your character over, and are trying to align the figure with the last frame captured!

The term "onion skinning" is borrowed from traditional cell animation, where drawings were made on thin see-through "onion-skin" paper, allowing the animator to see their previous drawings.

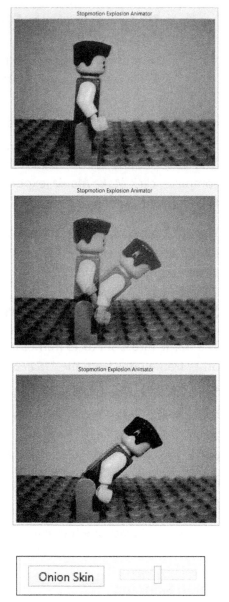

SME onion skin interface. The Onion Skin button activates the feature, and the slider fades between the live feed and last frame captured.

GLOSSARY

Animation Words

Frame rate (fps): The number of frames played per second in the finished animation. Higher frame rates (15-24 fps) will look smoother, but require more time to animate. Animations with lower frame rates (5-12 fps) are faster to create, but look "jerky."

Onion Skinning: Animation programs allow you to preview two frames at the same time, by making each frame transparent, and layering it on top of the previous frame.

Compression: Video files take up a lot of space on the computer's disk. Compression makes these files smaller. The software that accomplishes this is called a codec.

Codec: A codec is a piece of software for making a video file smaller., H.264 and MPEG-4 are popular codecs. Your animation program should allow you to pick from a list of codecs. You probably have several on your computer already, and many more are available as free downloads.

Saving a Project File

If you wish to save your animation for later work, click **File > Save**. This will allow you to save an XS file, which you can open later. You'll be prompted to save the project again before exiting, if you make any changes.

Note that you can't share your video with friends by sending them the project file. You'll need to export a video file first!

Creating a Movie File & Starting Over

Once you've created an animation and wish to export a video file for editing, or uploading to YouTube, click the **Make Movie** button. This will

Export Options

Output

Video Container: AVI

Select Codec: MPEG4

Codec Bitrate

Bitrate [Mbs]: 10.0

Cancel   Export

show the **Export Options** window. Here you can select the container format you prefer, a video codec, and adjust the quality of the video by moving the bitrate slider back and forth. A higher bitrate will result in a higher-quality image (Turn to the **Files and Formats** chapter for more information on this subject). For good compatibility with Windows Movie Maker, export AVI files with the MPEG-4 or H.264 codec.

When you click **Export**, the frames in the animation will play back, and a video file will be created. Now you can open the video file in the video player of your choice and watch the results. If you're happy with your creation, you can return to SME and click **File > New...** to begin a new animation. Or, you can click **Make Movie** and re-export the frames with different settings.

After clicking **File > New...**, you will be asked if you wish to save the animation to a project file. If you click **No**, you'll see a prompt showing the folder where the animation frames have been saved.

Saving a project file will allow you to reload the animation for additional work in the future. You can also load existing frames by importing them into the application.

Importing Frames

If you have a folder of pre-existing frames, you can import them by clicking *File > Import Frames...*

Before you import existing frames, you should set the camera resolution to match these frames. To quickly see the resolution of an existing frame, navigate to the folder that contains the frames, right-click an image in the sequence, and click the *Properties* option in the popup menu. The resolution can be found under the *Details* tab. Finally, click *Options > Camera Resolution...* in SME to match this resolution (more details on page 126).

After clicking *Import Frames...*, you will see this window. Clicking *Add Frames* will show a file dialog. Navigate to the folder of frames you wish to import. You can select some of or all the frames in the folder (use *Ctrl-A* to select all). Then click *Open*.

You will see the frames appear in the right half of the window. To import them into the animation, click the left-facing arrow, which will move them to the left side. The left side will also show any pre-existing animation frames.

125

By holding down the *Shift key + clicking*, you can select multiple frames on the left side, and then use the *Move Up* and *Move Down* buttons to adjust the order in which they play within the animation. You can also delete selected frames (which will not delete the original files, just the reference to them).

To save the changes you've made, click *Save Changes.*

Note that if you import frames before clicking the *Start / Grab* button, you will be asked to specify where the exported video file and new animation frames should be saved before you can begin animating.

Camera Settings & Resolution

To set the camera resolution, click *Options > Camera Resolution...*

Output Size:	Quality:		
1280 x 720 (default ∨			
	OK	Cancel	Apply

Output Size drop-down menu

This window allows you to select the resolution under the *Output Size* drop-down menu. Note that the other options in this menu will not effect the animation settings, only the image output from the camera. Animate at the largest resolution your computer can handle. You can scale your footage down to smaller resolutions afterwards.

To adjust the camera exposure, saturation, contrast and so on, click *Options > Capture Controls...* This will bring up a window with several tabs, allowing you to control and adjust the camera image.

Video Tutorial: SME Animator for OS X

To watch a video tutorial explaining how to use Stopmotion Explosion Animator for OS X, visit: *stopmotionexplosion.com/sme-osx*

Introduction to SME Animator for OS X

Stopmotion Explosion Animator for OS X is our frame-grabbing application for Mac users. While the interface differs from its Windows cousin, you'll find the same capture, playback, import, export and save functions in the app menus!

After starting up the program, you'll need to switch from your Mac's internal camera to the external animation camera (unless for some reason you want to use the computer's internal camera). Click and select the video input in the drop-down menu.

You should see the camera image appear in the two SME video windows. The window on the right is a preview of the frames that have been captured. The window on the left is a live image from the camera.

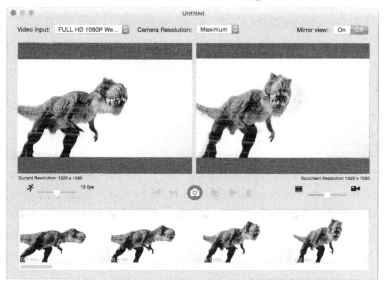

You may adjust the camera resolution by clicking the drop-down *Camera Resolution* menu. The options available will be limited by the camera connected to your computer. The current resolution is displayed in the bottom left corner of the screen.

Clicking the button that looks like a camera grabs a frame from your animation camera. You'll see the frames appearing in the filmstrip below the video windows.

If you tweak the slider underneath the right video window, you can adjust the amount of onion-skinning shown. The slider on the left adjusts the frame rate of the animation.

If you select a frame in the filmstrip by clicking it, you can delete this frame by clicking the button that looks like a trash can.

Finally, to export your animation, click *File > Export*. After typing in a name and clicking *Save*, you'll see a few codecs to choose from.

Codec setting: ● H264
                ○ JPEG

Quality setting: ● Normal quality
                  ○ High quality
                  ○ Low quality

                              Cancel   OK

If you're going to edit the film in iMovie, use *H.264* with the high quality setting. If you're planning to convert the footage into frames and add special effects, hit cancel. Click **File > Save...** and save a *.XPS* Stopmotion Explosion Animator Project File. If you right-click the project file and click "Show Package Contents", you'll see the frames of the animation saved as individual image files.

You can also double-click the project file to open and continue work on a previously created animation.

Miscellaneous Handy Stuff

Several small items are handy to have within reach while animating.

Tape

Very useful for securing objects that are prone to moving when they shouldn't. Buy the double-sided stuff if you can find it.

Blu-tac/Adhesive Putty

Like clay, except it's not oily and messy. Like tape, it's handy for keeping

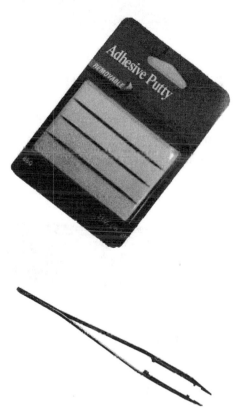

things in place. You can also stick it on the feet of your characters when they're walking on smooth surfaces or pulling off an acrobatic move, and need extra balance. Art supply stores carry this substance. Sometimes it's found in stationery aisles.

Tweezers

Handy for moving hard to reach objects in the far corners of your set, without bumping something with your fingers.

Poster board

Sheets in various natural colors make good backgrounds for your scenes. You can cut pieces into clouds, hills, and buildings.

Books, blocks of wood, flat things

These help you raise or lower a set or camera to get the angle you want.

Fun is Important!

Animating requires a lot of patience. Don't animate more than you're capable of in a day. Schedule time to unwind. Otherwise, you'll get sick of animating and loose your creative edge.

CHECK IT OUT!

Links

Stopmotion Explosion Animator for Windows / OS X:
stopmotionexplosion.com/downloads

Intelligent Filenames

The **Story** chapter discussed numbering scenes within the screenplay, and labeling frames in the storyboard with scene and shot numbers.

If you're working from a storyboard, you can name each video clip with the scene and shot number.

If you're animating from a script, name each video clip with the scene number and another number for the shot. Advance the shot number by 1 every time the camera is moved.

Finally, add a "take" number to the end of the filename. Takes are a simple way to track re-animated shots, if you animate a shot once, and decide to animate the same shot again, this is the second "take" of the shot, or "Take 2!"

In the end, you'll get something like this:

MyGreatMovie_Scene4_Shot1_Take1.avi

Looking at this name, we know it's the first take of the first shot in scene 4.

MyGreatMovie_Scene8_Shot3_Take1.avi

The first take of the third shot in scene 8, and so on…

Chapter 9

Flight

pecial effects in theatrical movies are created by skilled artists. They use sophisticated software, and elaborate equipment. We can achieve similar results with a little elbow grease and creativity.

The digital trickery in this chapter will be done with a paint program or image editor. The program you use must be better than Microsoft Paint. I have a couple of recommendations.

First, **Paint.NET.** The program is free, simple to use, and has many common image-editing tools. We'll be using Paint.NET in this chapter. OS X users will be happy to know that **Pinta**, a Paint.NET clone is available for the Mac. As of this writing, running Pinta currently requires installing the Mono framework.

GIMP is another free program with powerful features. It also comes in a Mac-compatible flavor. While I like GIMP for many reasons, if you can take advantage of Adobe's student discounts (which are also available to homeschoolers) I would recommend getting a copy of **Adobe Photoshop** and learning how to use it. It's an industry-standard skill which may provide you with a job someday.

134

At the end of the day, your image editor must have these basic features.

1 Layers. You should be able to stack multiple images on top of one another (more on this later).

2 An eraser tool.

Liftoff

The fasest, easiest way to fake small jumps is to have a character leap partly out of the picture with their first movement, then hold them in place with a pair of tweezers, or fingers. (Downside; you'll probably get your fingers in the picture, as shown here).

You can also use rigging to hold your object or character in the air while you animate their aerial antics.

Blank Frame

Before you start animating any action, capture a single frame of the background you want the character to fly across. This frame will be used to accomplish some digital trickery. (It could be the first or last frame of your animation sequence. We'll pull it out of the animation later).

Flying Rigs

After you've captured the blank frame, go ahead and animate your character flying through the air, held in place with your specially built flying rig. It's very important to make sure the lighting remains consistent throughout the animation, and the background isn't nudged or bumped.

Remember the frame rate and resolution of your animation. You'll need this information later.

Flying Rig Designs

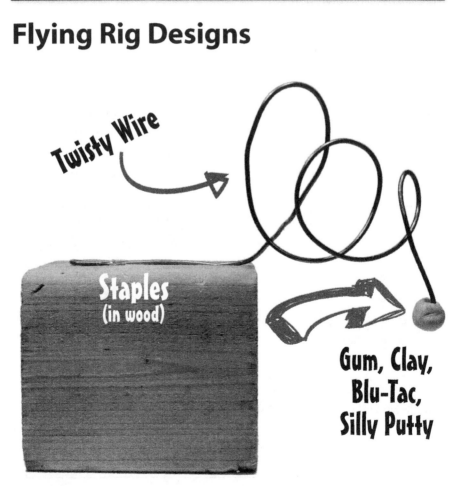

Twisty Wire

Staples
(in wood)

Gum, Clay,
Blu-Tac,
Silly Putty

Funky LEGO pieces

Stunt Guy

Helping Hands

Alligator Grip Clips

HOW TO

Flying Rig Techniques

Right   Wrong

The object to be animated should be attached to the rig in a place that's not visible from the camera's view.

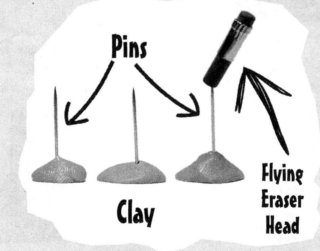

Pins

Clay

Flying Eraser Head

You can build rigs out of many things. Depending on the size of the object you're supporting, you could even build something out of pins.

Conversion

Finished the animation? The next step you take will vary, depending on how the animation program you're using saves frames to your computer.

1: Got Image Sequences?

If you're using a program that gives you the option to save individual image files instead of video files (Stopmotion Explosion Animator does this) you'll need to navigate to the directory the image files are saved in. Find this directory, then move on to step **3: File Numbers**.

2: Got Video Files?

If you're using a program that saves only video files, (the old SMA program does this) you'll need to convert the video file into a series of image files. Learn how to do this in the Frame Conversion chapter (look under the **Converting Video into Pictures** heading). Create the image files and save them somewhere on your computer. Move to **3: File Numbers**.

3: File Numbers

Number the images in the order they were captured while you were animating (i.e *frame001.jpg, frame002.jpg, frame003.jpg*). Most animation programs and video-to-image converters will do this automatically.

The first image in this sequence should be your blank image, the one you captured before you started animating.

Got your image files? Great. Let's start editing them!

I use Paint.NET in this example, but you can use any photo-editing program available, as long as the program supports layers, as I mentioned before.

Understanding Image Layers

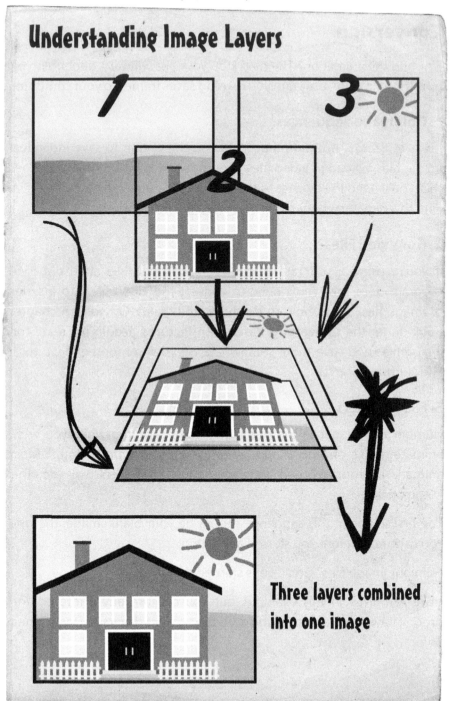

Three layers combined into one image

Layers

To understand how Paint.NET works, you'll need to understand layered images. It's really simple.

Imagine a painting on a sheet of glass. Now imagine a stack of three or four such paintings. Each painting is a "layer." The stack is sitting on a table, and you're looking at the painting on top.

If we erase half of the top painting, we'll be able to see the painting underneath through the glass. If we erase this painting, we'll see the third painting, and so on.

Take a look at the diagram I made to illustrate this concept. The layer workflow is something you'll encounter again and again, not only in image editors, but also in video compositing programs, and video editors.

Begin the Edit

Start up Paint.NET, or the image editor of your choice.

First, we'll create a new image. Click **File > New**.

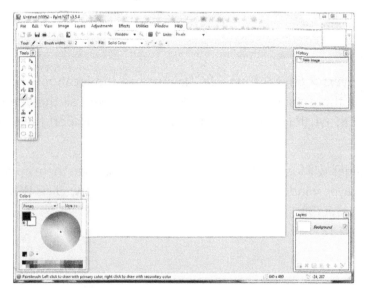

Stopmotion Explosion

Video Tutorial: Paint.NET

To watch a video tutorial explaining how to make a LEGO® Minifig fly in Paint.NET, visit: *stopmotionexplosion.com/flight*

Set the resolution of the image to the resolution of the image files you will be editing. My images have a width of **640**, and a height of **480**. Leave everything else at the default settings.

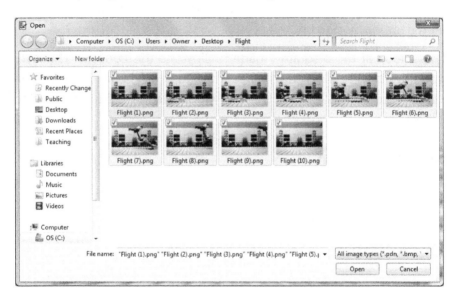

Click **Layers > Import from File**. Navigate to the location where you saved all those animation image files earlier. Select all the images by hitting **Ctrl +A**. (If you're using Pinta, you'll have to import them one at a time).

The images will load into Paint.NET as layers. You'll see them appearing in the Layer window. (If you don't see this window, click **Window > Layers**, or hit **F7**).

Familiarize yourself with this window, because you'll be using it a lot. Uncheck all the layers except the first two layers, and the bottom **background** layer. You can see how I've done so here.

As mentioned earlier, I've numbered the layers in the order they appeared in the original animation.

- The "Flight (1)" layer is the frame with nothing in it, the frame I captured before starting to animate with the flying rig.

Layers in the Layers Window

- "Flight (2)" is the first frame with the flying rig.

- The *background* frame is a blank, white frame with nothing in it. You can ignore this layer.

On the left side of the paint program, you should see a window with paint tools. If not click **Window > Tools**, or hit **F5**. Click the **Eraser** tool.

Tool: ✏ ▾ | Brush width: ⊟ 40 ▾ ⊕

You'll need to adjust the width of the eraser, so you're not erasing tiny dots. Adjust the brush width until it's medium sized.

Return to the Layers window. Click the second layer, so it's highlighted as in the picture. This is important.

In the image window, you should see your "flying" character, and some of the rig supporting him in the air. Let's erase the rig!

Click, and start erasing. Erase until the rig is completely gone. Pretty amazing huh?

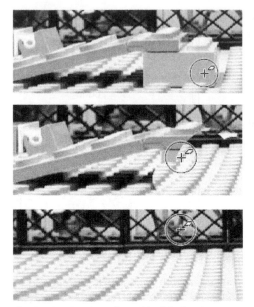

Erasing the rig. Adjust the width of the brush to erase the tricky spots, where the rig touches the character.

Save this image by clicking *File > Save As...*

Here's where things get a little wonky. In the *Save as type* drop-down menu, click *JPG*. This is the first frame of our flight animation, so name it *"AnimationFlight_1.jpg"* or something similar. Numbering your saved frames is very important, as this will allow you to re-assemble them into a video file later! Click *Save*. You might get a *Save Configuration* window. Go with the default settings and click OK.

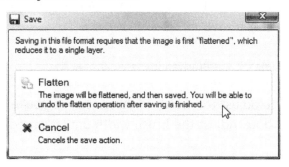

You'll see this window appear. Click *Flatten*. The image will save... but HEY! Where did all our layers go?

A document "flattened" to just one layer.

Don't worry. They're still hanging around. Click *Edit > Undo*, and the layers will pop back like they never left.

If you're using a program like Photoshop, you'll be able to "save a copy," which saves a JPG file without an extra step.

GLOSSARY

Computer Graphics

Bit: One digit of a number stored in a computer. It can be either 1 or 0. Most computers now store a color as a 24 bit number—8 bits for the amount of red, 8 for green and 8 for blue. This is called "RGB24" color.

Bitmap / BMP: Contains the bits that stand for the colors of every pixel in a picture, arranged in order starting at one corner. The files contain a lot of information and are very large.

JPEG & PNG: Contain bits that represent the colors in a picture. Instead of one bit for every pixel, the bits may stand for areas of color or for changes between a pixel and the pixels surrounding it. This makes the filesize much smaller.

Unfortunately, Paint.NET doesn't have this feature, so we'll be using the aforementioned workaround (also note: you won't see these steps if you're using Pinta!)

Next step. In the Layer window, uncheck the layer you just edited, and check the layer immediately above it. Make sure the layer is selected by clicking it, as pictured.

Go ahead and erase the rig in this image. Make sure you're cleaning up any shadows, and pay special attention to areas where the rig goes behind your character, or intersects with it.

Save, following the steps of the workaround mentioned previously, and continue on to the next layer.

To edit the next layer, you must make sure it is "checked"

If you're having problems erasing parts of the layer, (you erase, and erase, but nothing happens) chances are, you haven't selected the layer first, by clicking it in the Layers panel. You can only edit a layer if it's selected!

Erase the rig in all the frames of your animation. You can zoom in and out with the magnifying glass tool, and adjust the width of the eraser for finer control. If you mess up and erase the wrong thing, hit *Ctrl+Z* or *apple + Z* on OS X.

Conversion Take Two

After you finish erasing the rig in every image, you'll have a folder of edited images. If you've followed the instructions so far, you've numbered them in the order they appear. The last step is converting the images into a video file. This can be done easily with a frame conversion program. Turn to the **Frame Conversion** chapter for more information about this.

This compositing technique has many uses. Instead of using the eraser, as I did in this example, you could use a paint tool, and draw explosions, or graphic effects on frames. You can remove the background from pictures of objects and place the object into your animation. With a little practice, it's possible to composite moving mouths and expressions on characters.

If you find yourself compositing a lot of frames, you should move to a dedicated video compositing program, like **After Effects,** or **DebugMode's Wax 2.0** (a free program).

Chroma Key Effects

Chroma-keying is another way to create the appearance of flight.

You may have seen blue and green screens placed behind actors and objects in movie studios. The chroma-key effect is used to place a TV weatherman in front of huge radar displays, and insert model planes and spaceships in the sky.

146

Before

After

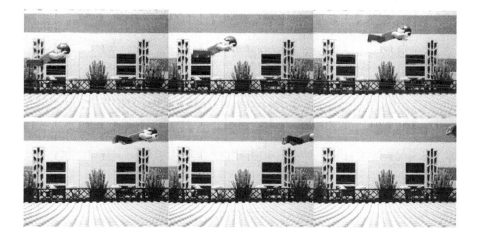

Some video editors come with a chroma-key effect that can be applied to footage with a green or blue background. **Windows Movie Maker 6.0**, the free editing program for Windows can do some basic chroma-keying, but it requires downloading and installing a user-made effect (visit the Stopmotion Explosion video tutorial link in this chapter for more information about this). Chroma keying is also possible with the **iMovie** application for OS X.

Shoot footage with a solid blue background behind your figure. You can choose green as well. Pick a color that is different from all the colors in the object you wish to chroma key (i.e. if the object is blue, use a green background!)

Video Tutorials: Chroma Keying

Learn how to chroma key in iMovie and Windows Movie Maker!

stopmotionexplosion.com/chromakey-imovie

stopmotionexplosion.com/chromakey-wmm

Choose a scene you want behind the character. This can be a still picture, graphic, or a live video clip.

Place your bluescreen clip and the clip you wish to appear behind your character on the video editor's timeline. Video editors with chroma-key abilities often have two or more video tracks. You'll place the bluescreen clip on the top track, and the second clip on the bottom track.

Select the chroma-key effect and apply it to the bluescreen clip. The effect analyzes the footage and makes solid colors transparent. In this example, all blue color in the clip will become transparent, revealing the new background behind your character.

Study your video editor's manual to learn more of the chroma key's controls and parameters. These will improve the quality of your "key." Check out the video tutorials on the Stopmotion Explosion website for

CHECK IT OUT!

Links

Paint.NET
www.getpaint.net

Pinta
www.pinta-project.com

GIMP
www.gimp.org

Wax 2.0
www.debugmode.com/wax/

more information about chroma keying in iMovie and Windows Movie Maker.

The free Wax 2.0 compositing program is often recommended for basic chroma key operations. You can find many tutorials for using the program on YouTube, and the Internet.

Chapter 10

The Art of War

Choreography is made of two words, the greek *Khoreia* which means "choral dance" and *Graphia*, Latin for "writing." Dance choreographers compose steps in ballet. Fight choreographers compose moves in a fight.

Fight Arc Graph

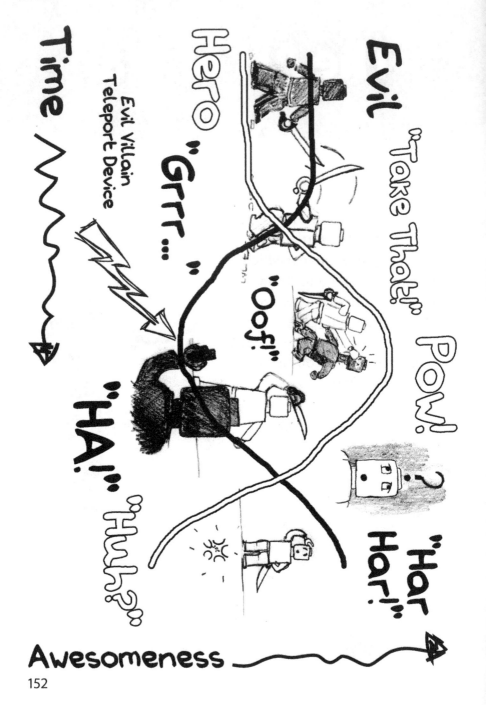

Though the action in a movie fight looks spontaneous, every move is carefully planned and rehearsed by the choreographers, like a performance of the Swan Lake Ballet!

Think about dancing. If two people are dancing together, one makes a movement and their partner responds. Fighting is very similar. One person throws a punch, and their opponent reacts by blocking, dodging, or returning the blow.

As a choreographer, you'll decide what weapons and fighting styles are used, how long the fight lasts, and how the fight will arc from beginning to end.

Arcs are simple to understand. Take a look at one here.

The best stories use conflict to help the audience understand the hero and villain. The hero loses his first battles because he's flawed. Maybe he's over confident, or doesn't understand the problem he's facing. The villain is really evil and tough to beat. After being defeated several

CHECK IT OUT!

Story Arc

Here is a graph of a duel between an evil genius scientist, and a white-suited hero, of average intelligence. On the graph, time is plotted horizontally, awesomeness vertically.

As the hero gets the upper hand, his level of awesomeness goes up. The villain's arc of awesomeness starts going down.

Just when it looks like the villain will be defeated, he reveals his secret teleporter. The villain's arc goes up, and the hero's arc goes down, just as the episode ends. Tune in next time...

times, the hero "gets it," addresses his fatal flaws, and comes back to win.

Take another look at the fight arc. Do you think the conflict between the hero and villain has been resolved?

You've Got Moves

Punches and kicks should be exaggerated. There's anticipation, as the figure prepares to throw the punch, they pull their arm back. The punch itself moves quickly, and is followed with a few frames of slow movement, as the figure recovers from the punch.

Break each movement of a fight sequence into a single segment that can be re-animated several times if needed. It may take some experimentation to perfect the right balance of anticipation, swing, reaction, and recovery.

Movement-challenged figures should be animated with a lot of anticipation and follow-through. For example, in the following breakdowns, notice how the minifig throws his whole body into a punch. The same applies to a minifig taking a punch. They react with their whole body.

Check out some breakdowns over the next few pages. Stikfas are used in a few instances, but the same movements can be duplicated with any multi-jointed figure.

Right Body Strike

Suit Guy is knocked back, arms trailing as he flies. Landing, he slides slightly.

Uppercut

White Ninja bops Suit Guy on the chin.

Left Hook

Suit Guy comes around with the punch. Notice slight White Ninja reaction before impact.

Right Body Strike

Simple, straight punch. The punched character's head should snap back, as shown here.

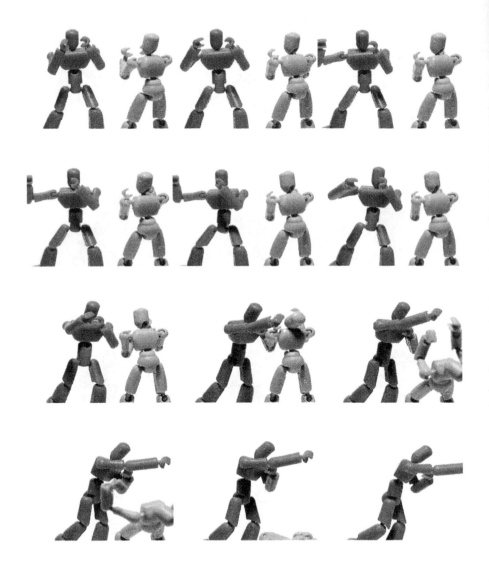

Roundhouse Kick

Roundhouse kick to the back. Double-sided tape is extremely useful for these poses.

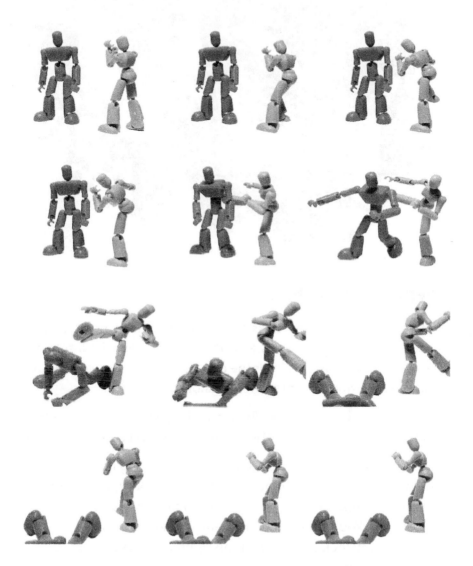

Keeping it Real Fake

Most of the punches and kicks thrown by stuntman don't connect. Instead, their opponent reacts as if they've been punched, snapping their body backwards. This saves the producers lots of hospital bills, and keeps the performers alive for another show.

You're working with toys and figures that don't care if they've been punched. Should they pummel each other with everything they've got?

Maintaining the speed of a punch will require spacing between frames that doesn't allow a fist or foot (or tentacle/claw/beak) to connect in a frame. This is especially true if you're animating at a lower frame rate, say 10-15 FPS. You'll be animating a frame immediately *after* a punch connects. If you look at frame 8 of the Uppercut breakdown, you'll see an excellent example of a non-connecting punch.

What's the solution to this dilemma? Sound effects!

Sound Effects

Comic books have BAM! and POW! inked in big, bold letters because...

A punch needs to SOUND like a punch!

This applies to animated and live action films too. That crisp "POW" from the Lone Ranger's fist is a recording of someone punching a raw steak with a leather glove (for extra slap). No kiddin'. Sound effects add extra weight to fighting action. Be sure to sprinkle a generous helping into the mix while editing your film. (Learn about sound in the next chapter).

Explosions

A thug pulls out his pocket RPG. The hero swings his katana just in time to deflect the missile, which skips across the ground and collides with a propane truck sitting under a critical fuel supply line. How will you animate all that boom?

In today's live-action films, explosions are filmed on site, composited in after filming, or created with a combination of both methods. For many years, stopmotion was used primarily for creating effects in live action films, including explosions. Here are some helpful tips for animating explosions in your own productions using odds and ends from around the house.

Black & White

Capture one bright over-exposed frame, then one under-exposed frame immediately before animating the body of an explosion. Point a light directly into the camera for the light frame, or crank the exposure up. Turn all the set lights off for the dark frame or cover the camera lens. This is a traditional cartooning technique, and adds extra punch to an explosion.

Cotton Wool

You can buy bags of little cotton balls at cosmetic shops, or "quilt batting" from craft stores. This fluffy stuff forms the explosion cloud. Pull the cotton apart, slowly adding more in each frame until the explosion is big enough, then continue pulling the cotton apart and removing pieces until it drifts out of the frame. Check out the frame-by-frame .ample in this chapter.

Flashlight

Flashlights are useful for creating the glowing heart of an explosion. You can use them with cotton (point the light in the middle of the cloud) or create small spot explosions without the cloud.

Cotton Wool Smoke Breakdown

Example: The Rocket

Five...four...three...two...one... wait! Your moon explorers are grounded if their rocket doesn't have some propellant! This simple effect will get them to the stars and back again.

Build a rocket with a hollow body. Cardboard tubes work well. Use tape or wire to attach your rocket to a flashlight, with the flashlight pointing down, through the rocket body (see illustration).

Turn the flashlight on. Hold your "rocket" by the flashlight handle. Start capturing frames and raising the rocket into the air. Use cotton smoke below the rocket to enhance the effect.

Paper

Paper cutouts can be used to create small explosions. Grab a sheet of card stock, construction paper, or poster board, if your cutout will be very large.

Create several cutouts of progressing size, one for each stage of the explosion, and insert the cutouts into the scene, one frame at a time, starting with the smallest and ending with the largest.

Here's an animation of a water main breaking, made with six construction-paper cutouts (check out the breakdown in this chapter). Note how the animation alternates between two cutouts in the last six frames, creating the illusion of leaping water.

Papermation Water Spray Breakdown

Gunfire

Firing a gun creates muzzle flash, a small explosion from the tip of the gun. The gun kicks back, moving the gunman's arm slightly each time it's fired.

You can animate a muzzle flash and the arm movement using a combination of the techniques I've introduced so far. These effects should be visible for about one frame, if you're animating at 15 FPS. Add a gunshot sound effect during the edit.

Flashlight Blast

Really basic. A flashlight pointed into the set for one or two frames. Combining this technique with the other effects here will produce a better effect.

Paper Blast

A paper cutout of a muzzle flash. Post-it notes are great for this. Cut the flash out of the post-it so that the sticky part is the end that attaches to the muzzle of the gun.

Cotton Blast

The blast of a black powder flintlock pistol, with cotton wool smoke. Use a little glue from a glue stick to attach the wool to the muzzle. The "smoke" should be visible for several frames, appearing quickly, as the gun is fired, and slowly drifting away afterwards.

Enhanced Blast

I've made the flashlight blast a little more impressive by drawing a muzzle flash into the frame with Paint.NET. Learn about this on page 171.

LEGO® Blaster

When you visit galaxies far, far away, everyone is packing their favorite blaster-gas projectile accessory. If you're animating with a construction toy, you can use a long thin piece for the blaster beam, like this transparent LEGO® antenna. Since the piece is visible for a single frame, it will look like a "real" laser beam.

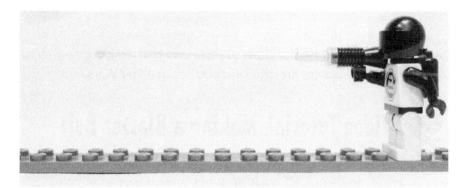

Knitting Needle Blaster

You can use any long, thin object as a blaster beam, like knitting needles. Use your fingers, or another character to support the other end of the needle off-screen.

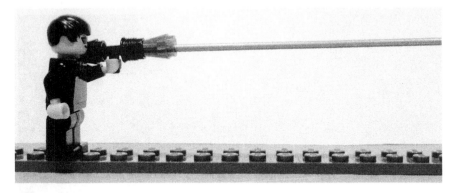

Paint.NET Blaster

I introduced Paint.NET in the previous chapter, showing how to create the illusion of flight by erasing supports using the program's layers and image-editing tools.

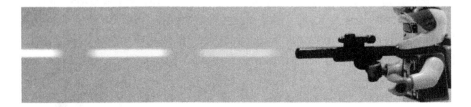

You can also use Paint.NET to draw objects into frames. Here's a way to draw and animate blaster fire, the kind you see in a Star Wars film.

Video Tutorial: Making a Blaster Bolt

To watch a video tutorial explaining how to create blaster bolts in Paint.NET, visit: *stopmotionexplosion.com/scifi*

PROJECT

Creating Blaster FX

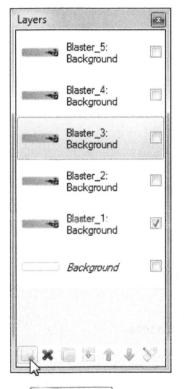

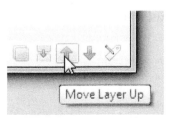

Read the introduction to Paint.NET on page 141, if you haven't done so already. Following the tutorial, convert your animation into frames (if needed), start Paint.NET, create a new image with the same resolution as your animation, import your images as layers and hide all the layers except the one containing the first frame of your animation.

1 At the bottom of the Layers window, click the "Add New Layer" button, which looks like a little square with a plus mark on the corner.

This will add a new blank layer to the stack of layers in the Layer window. We need to move this layer to the top of the stack.

2 Select the new layer by clicking it, and click the little arrow pointing up, until the new layer is on top.

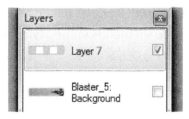

PROJECT

3 Finally, double-click this new layer (pictured as **Layer 7**) and rename it "Blaster Layer" in the Layer Properties window.

Now it's time to draw the blaster bolt.

4 In the *Colors* window, pick a nice blue. If you don't see this window, click the colors icon in the top right corner.

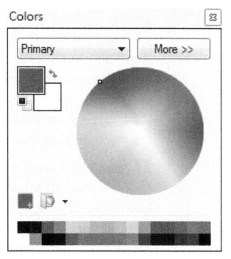

5 In the Tools window, click the *Lines / Curves* tool.

6 We want the line to look like a blaster bolt. The ends should be rounded, and the width of the bolt should be roughly the same as the width of the blaster muzzle.

In this example, I've made the width of the brush 35 pixels, and set both ends of the line to be rounded using the two drop-down menus in the *Style* area

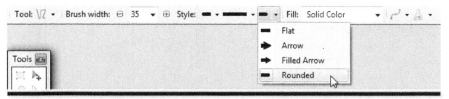

7 To draw the bolt, click and drag the mouse in a straight line away from the blaster muzzle. The length of the bolt is entirely up to you.

Holding the *Shift* key down while you drag the mouse will draw a perfectly straight line.

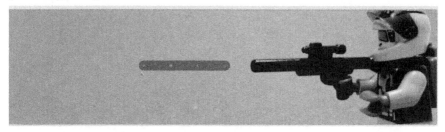

8 A blaster bolt has a white-hot center surrounded by a colored corona (an effect caused by superheated particles releasing energy into the environment as light!) We'll blur the edges of the line we just drew, creating the corona, and recolor the center for that white-hot effect. Click *Effects > Blur > Gaussian Blur...*

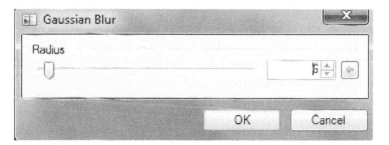

Use enough blur to make the edges of the bolt fuzzy. I've set a radius of 6 pixels, but you can experiment. Click *OK*.

9 Now, click *Effects > Photo > Glow*.

PROJECT

> **Glow**   ×
>
> Radius
>
> Brightness   100
>
> Contrast   100
>
> OK   Cancel

Crank the Brightness and Contrast up to 100, giving the bolt a white center. Set the radius to around 3 pixels, so a nice rim of blue is visible around the edge of the bolt.

You can increase the amount of glow by clicking *Effects > Repeat Glow...* but this may decolor the corona.

10 Finally, (you can skip this step, but it makes the bolt look nicer) add some motion blur. Click *Effects > Blurs > Motion Blur...*

Set the angle of the blur to be the direction the bolt is traveling. Our bolt is traveling straight across the screen, so the angle is 0. If the bolt was traveling straight towards

> Motion Blur   ✕
>
> Angle   0.00
>
> ☑ Centered
>
> Distance   51
>
> OK   Cancel

the top of the screen, we would set the angle to 90. To set the angle correctly, simply drag the line inside the Angle circle around so the line is pointing in the direction the bolt is moving.

The distance of the blur in pixels should be great enough to leave a nice "tail" around the bolt. Try a value of 40-50. It might take a few seconds to render the blur.

11 Why not add a little muzzle flash too? To create the effect below, make a new layer, paint over the muzzle using a large white brush, and apply the Gaussian Blur filter to the layer (*Effects > Blur > Gaussian Blur...*), with a radius of 45 pixels. The flash is visible for one frame.

12 One frame of our blaster bolt animation is complete. Save the frame by clicking *File > Save As...*

If you followed the Paint.NET tutorial prior to reading this chapter, you'll remember there's a trick to saving images in Paint.NET. In the *Save as type* drop-down menu, click *JPG*. This is the first frame of our blaster animation. Name it *"Blaster_Fire01.JPG."* Don't forget to number the frames as you save them!

PROJECT

Click **Save**. You might see a **Save Configuration** window. Go with the default settings and click **OK**.

This window will appear. Click **Flatten**. The image will save, and your layers will disappear. Click **Edit > Undo**, and they'll pop back again.

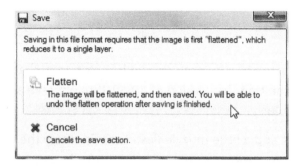

Paint.NET, and most image and video programs that use layers allow the position of a layer to be adjusted independently of all the other layers. This is very useful. Instead of drawing a new blaster bolt ahead of the bolt we just created and erasing the old one, we can move the old blaster bolt forward, and save the results!

1 3 Creating the next frame of the animation is very simple. Hide the current frame, the one we just exported, by un-checking the checkbox next to it in the Layer window. Reveal the next frame by checking its box. Leave the box next to the Blaster Layer checked (see illustration).

1 4 In the Tools window, click the **Move Selected Pixels** button. Make sure the blaster layer is selected by clicking it. Click the blaster bolt somewhere in the middle. Drag the bolt forward, releasing it when it's roughly twice the distance away from the muzzle it was in the previous frame. You can also hold down the control key, and move the bolt with the right and left arrow keys.

1 5 Save this frame, following the previously outlined steps. Move the blaster bolt forward in each frame in your animation. When you are finished, assemble the individual frames into a movie file using a image-to-video converter. Check out the **Frame Conversion** chapter for more information about this.

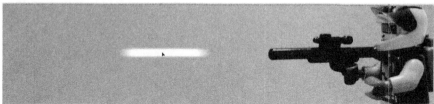

1 6 If you are animating more than one blaster bolt in a frame of your animation, draw each bolt on a separate layer. You can customize blaster bolts by drawing the initial line in different colors. I used blue. Try yellow, red and green.

An Elegant Weapon

This technique can also be used to create lightsaber effects.

First, animate your figures battling with solid, straight rods. Draw the lightsaber "blade" over the rods. Draw each blade on a different layer. The layer with the blade closest to the camera should be on top.

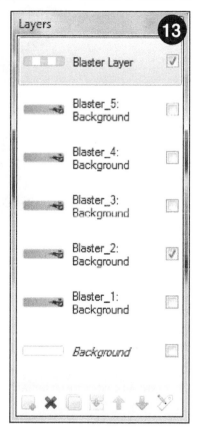

When the blades clash, insert a white frame, then a black frame, and finally, paint in a large flash with the same gaussian blur method used to create a blaster muzzle flash. This flash should last a couple of frames.

Chapter 11

Sound

Straight from the camera, stopmotion films have no audio. This is a problem, because we aren't living in the 1920s, and you want sound effects and characters with voices in your movies!

This chapter contains fancy techniques for recording and editing sound. If you're looking to add sounds to an animation you've made, read this chapter until Audacity is introduced, then page ahead to the Video Editing chapter, where you will find specific instructions for adding sound to animation.

Microphones

Many computers have built-in microphones. This microphone can be a great solution for your first film; however it's preferable to use a microphone that plugs into your computer. Doing so will allow you to bring the microphone closer to sound sources and voices.

If you have access to a regular PA style microphone, you can acquire an adapter that converts the three-prong microphone connector into the computer's miniature audio connector. Additionally, USB XLR interfaces can be purchased. This is basically a box that sits between the microphone and computer. The microphone's XLR cable plugs into the box, and the box interfaces with the computer via USB.

Once your microphone is plugged in, you can launch your audio recording program. For starters, try using the **Windows Sound Recorder,**

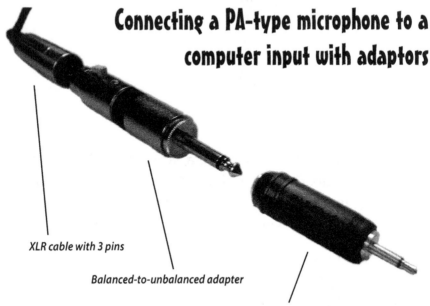

Connecting a PA-type microphone to a computer input with adaptors

XLR cable with 3 pins

Balanced-to-unbalanced adapter

1/4 inch to 1/8 inch adapter

If you don't have a microphone, visit the nearest computer store, or hit eBay. Microphones for Windows and Mac systems are inexpensive and easy to find.

which comes with all Windows installations, typically found in the **Start** menu, under **Accessories**. You can also record sound with the **Windows Movie Maker** program (turn to the Video Editing chapter for more on this).

If you've ever used a tape recorder, Sound Recorder doesn't need much explanation. Click the round record button to start recording sound. Click *Stop Recording* to stop, and save a sound file.

If your sound is very quiet, or sounds bad, try increasing the volume, or changing settings in the **Hardware and Sound** section of the Windows control panel.

OS X users can use the **GarageBand** application or **iMovie** to record sounds from their microphone, or the free **Audacity** program. I've included instructions for using Audacity at the end of this chapter.

Recording Sessions

When professional sound crew scout a location for problems, they listen for nearby traffic, look for refrigerators to unplug, and worry about water running through pipes. A real recording studio has carefully placed blocks of foam to minimize echo, and special soundproof recording booths.

Your recording equipment may not be very sensitive, especially if you're recording sound with the computer's built-in microphone, but you should still try to isolate yourself from unwanted noise. Find a quiet environment to work in.

Recording Sound Effects

If you purchase an MP3 recorder, or MP3 player with an internal microphone, you can record sounds anywhere. Audacity's effects, which you'll learn how to use later, can transform boring sounds into amazing exotic mutations. Here are a few ideas to get you started:

- **Punch** - Pile of jackets and gloves hit with baseball bat. You can hit many objects with sticks, bats, and record great sounds.
- **Snakes Slithering** - Fingers run through cheese casserole.
- **Rock Rolling** - Car coasting, pitch lowered.
- **Rats** - Chickens, sped up.
- **Earth Cracking** - Balloons rubbed together, pitch lowered.
- **Fire** - Crackling cellophane mixed with sticks snapping.
- **Ghosts** - Dolphins sounds sped up.
- **Large Explosion** - Wind rumble (blowing into mic), pitch lowered.
- **Elevator Door** - File cabinet drawer (add bell ding).
- **Bird Wings** - Leather gloves flapping.
- **Snow** - Carpet laid over gravel, corn starch in container.
- **Monster** - Slide straw in and out of McDonald's cup, pitch lowered.
- **Sword Swoosh** - Spin a rope through the air, past the microphone. Sticks can also be used.
- **Large Crash** - Set tin cans and other noisemaking items on stepladder stairs, tip them over.
- **Baseball hit** - Match snapping, pitch lowered.

Speeding up or slowing down a sound raises and lowers the pitch, which makes the sound high and squeaky, or low and deep. The pitch can also be adjusted independently of the audio speed using software effects.

It might be tough to record dolphins yourself. Not to worry. Check out some of the sound effect resources at the end of this chapter.

Recording Dialog

Grab your script and some voice talent. Family and friends are great sources of talent, especially if they enjoy reading books aloud with all the character's voices, or walk around the house repeating quotes from their favorite films.

It's not ideal to have a crowd of people huddled around one microphone saying their lines. It's better to record one character's lines individually, then move to the next character. This will reduce noise, and allow each performer to get close to the microphone.

While recording, listen to your talent. Coach them, and make sure all their lines are being said with the right expressions. It can be helpful to play the animation at the same time, to better match your talent's lines to the character's actions.

Leave little pauses between each line. This will make your sound files easier to edit later.

Once you're finished a character's lines, stop recording. Use the rewind and play controls to preview the recording. Ensure it sounds the way you want. Save the recording and begin the next character's lines.

After the recording session, when the sound files you created are imported into your editing program, you'll be able to split the recordings into individual lines and place each line where it's needed, in relation to your animation.

Some will suggest recording all your characters' lines first, then animating to match the character's voices. Others suggest animating first, then recording dialog to match the animation. If you're animating characters with moving lips, you'll need to record the dialog first. Otherwise, it's your decision to make.

Preventing Plosives

Proper microphone placement can prevent common recording problems. Have you ever heard an audio recording that sounded like this?

"We have PHFFete on the scene, rePPHForting on the PHFFerfect... PUHF PUFH..."

These glitches called "plosives" result when a microphone is too close to the speaker. The "P" sound creates a gust of air, resulting in the bad audio.

To avoid this problem, keep the microphone a distance from the speaker, and point it at their chest, rather than their lips. Foam windscreens placed over the mic can also prevent plosive-explosions.

Music

More than any other sound element, music connects directly with our emotions. Music can transform daily life into a gripping adventure, or a short goodbye into a heartbreaking farewell.

If you're making movies and showing them to a limited circle of family and friends, you can use CD tracks and downloaded music in your films. If you upload films with copyrighted music to the Internet, there is a chance the video will be removed, or the audio muted. Take time to research potential copyright and ownership issues if you choose to share your productions with a public audience. Turn to page 253 for more information about this.

Audio Editing with Audacity

After you've worked with audio for a while, you might want to create more complicated sounds. If so, you'll want to check out Audacity, a free open-source sound editing program. Audacity and similar programs allow you to record, edit, and enhance sounds by combining multiple sound tracks (download link at end of this chapter).

You can use Audacity's many effects to add an echo to your recordings, or raise the pitch of a sound higher or lower. You can remove audio glitches as well.

We'll use Audacity to record a voice, change the voice so it sounds like a chipmunk, and save the voice as a sound file that can be used in a movie.

Video Tutorial: Audio & Effects

Watch a video tutorial explaining Audacity on our site!
stopmotionexplosion.com/audacity

First, plug your microphone into the computer, and move into a suitably quiet environment. Start up Audacity. You'll see a window like the one pictured. Now, look at the upper left corner:

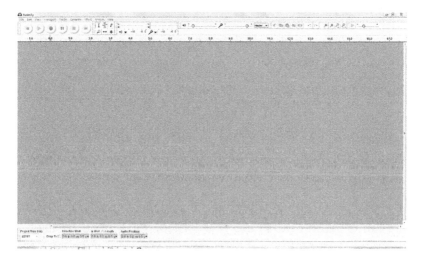

Familiarize yourself with these controls, because you'll be using them over and over again. If you forget what a button does, hover over the button with your mouse cursor, and a little reminder box will pop up.

Immediately to the right of the round control buttons, you'll see a collection of funny symbols. These are "tools" you'll use to manipulate and edit the audio in various ways.

185

Also in the toolbar are two **audio meters**.

Audio meters show a little bar that jumps up and down as you record and play sound. The louder the sound is, the higher the bar jumps.

Recording Audio

Let's record a line of dialog. Make sure your microphone is plugged in. Hit the round red *Record* button. Say the following line:

"Hi, my name is Hammy the Hamster, and my voice sounds really squeaky. Hee hee hee!"

As you speak, you'll notice two things. First, the audio meter on the far right will be bouncing up and down. Secondly, a long blue squiggly line will appear in an audio track below the record button.

Note: If your microphone is plugged in, yet you do not see the audio meters jumping, and no sound is recorded, you'll need to select the correct audio input. Click the drop-down menu, or arrow next to the microphone symbol.

When you finish saying your lines, hit the square *Stop* button. You've recorded your first sound! To play your recording back, hit the triangular *Play* button. If you really hate your recording, click the little **x** button next

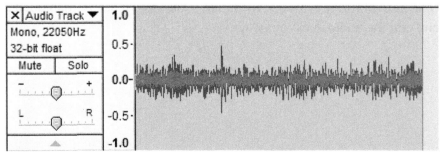

to **Audio Track**, and repeat the steps above until you have a recording you're happy with.

Let's go ahead and save our audio session. Click *File > Save Project...* and give the project a name, like "Hammy." If Audacity crashes, we'll have a backup of our recording. Keep saving as we move forward!

Let's edit this recording. You probably recorded a few seconds of silence before saying Hammy's lines. Let's trim this silence out of the clip.

Waveforms

Look at those blue squiggly lines again. These lines are called "Waveforms." The smaller these "waves" are, the quieter the sound is. If the waveforms are loud, the waveforms will be big. If the sound is too loud, the waveforms will be so big, they clip, going outside the boundaries of the track. This isn't good.

Selecting and Deleting Audio

At the start of the track, you'll see a short section of very small waveforms. If you click *Play* and watch the track, you'll notice the sound is silent here. Let's remove this section.

In the tools area, click the tool that looks like a capitol I. Click the audio track, just after the small waveforms end (where the black line is in the illustration).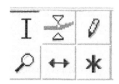

You'll notice a small vertical line has appeared where you clicked. If you hover over this line with your mouse, you'll notice the mouse cursor changing into a hand with a finger pointing left.

Click and hold the mouse button, dragging all the way back to the beginning of the recording, and release the mouse button. This will select all the audio up to the vertical line.

Alternatively, instead of clicking and dragging, you can click anywhere in the track and hit **Shift + J**. This will select all the audio from the beginning of the track to the vertical line.

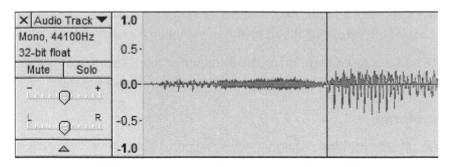

To remove the selected audio, click **Edit > Delete**, or hit **Ctrl + K**. Zing! The audio is gone.

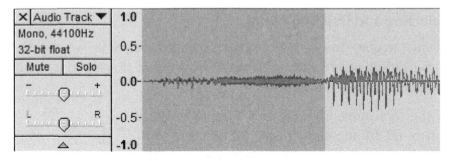

If you have a few seconds of silent audio at the end of your track too, you can remove it using the same method. Click and drag with the **I** tool until the end of the track, or click in one spot and hit **Ctrl + J** to select all the audio from the end of the track to the line.

You can also select and remove sections of audio in the middle of a recording by clicking and dragging anywhere in the track with the **I** tool. This is useful for removing unwanted pops, bumps, and rumbles.

If you're having trouble viewing all of the track at once, click the tool that looks like a magnifying glass, hold down the *Shift* key, and click the track. Zoom in by clicking the track with this tool, without holding down the *Shift* key.

HEADS UP

Backup!

If you want to back up an Audacity project to a hard drive, or CD, you'll have to copy two files, the project's .aup file, and associated data folder.

For example, our project has a project file, "Hammy.aup" and a file of audio data, "Hammy_data" that must be copied to your backup disk.

Save your project. Let's go ahead and add the chipmunk effect to our voice.

Effect: Change Pitch

Click *Edit > Select > Select All*, or hit *Ctrl + A* to select the entire recording. Alternatively, you can click immediately below the words "Audio Track" to select the track.

Now, click *Effect > Change Pitch...*

If you've ever messed around with a cassette player, you may have figured out how to hit the fast-forward button so the tape played really fast, and everything sounded squeaky, like a chipmunk band.

If we changed the speed of our recording, the sound would play back faster, in a shorter amount of time. We don't want this. Instead of playing the sound faster, we're simply changing the pitch of the sound, so everything sounds higher.

Here's the pitch effect window and parameters.

To change the pitch higher, grab the slider and drag it to the right. To change the pitch lower, drag to the left. To hear a sample of the effect, click *Preview*. When you're happy with the results, click *OK*.

Effect: Change Speed

If you really want to change the speed AND pitch of your recording, hit *Cancel* above, and click *Effect > Change Speed...* Drag the slider up and down, laughing hilariously at your goofy voice. Finally, click *OK*.

Saving a WAV File

We are done! Let's export an audio file that can be used in our movie projects.

Click *File > Export...* You'll see a Save File dialog pop up. Give the file a name. In the *Save as Type* drop-down menu, click *"WAV (Microsoft) signed 16 bit PCM."* Click *Save*.

File name:	Hammy	▼	Save
Save as type:	WAV (Microsoft) signed 16 bit PCM	▼	Cancel
			Options...

The Save File Pop-Up Dialog

You may see another window pop up, asking you to label the file with some additional data. This is a useful way to organize your files. You can see I've filled out the fields with some information pertaining to this recording. Click **OK** when you're done.

Edit Metadata   ☒

Use arrow keys (or RETURN key after editing) to navigate fields.

Tag	Value
Artist Name	Joe Soundguy
Track Title	
Album Title	Hammy the Hamster
Track Number	
Year	2010
Genre	Vocal
Comments	

Add   Remove   Clear

Genres   Template

Edit...   Reset...   Load...   Save...   Set Default

OK   Cancel

Congratulations! You've recorded, edited, and saved a line of dialog for your film. The process I've outlined above can be applied to any sound you record.

This chapter has just scratched the surface of the many things you can accomplish with Audacity. I encourage you to experiment with the program and its tools and effects.

Audio Files

The **Wave** file is a very common sound format. Wave files have a **.WAV** extension.

You may be able to create **MP3** or **WMA** files with your recording software. These formats were designed to reduce the size of audio recordings, making them easier to download and upload, with a slight loss in audio quality.

Free Sound Effects

If you're looking for free, downloadable sound effects, create an account with **The Freesound Project**:

freesound.org

Hundreds of sound hobbyists upload their creations to this site under the Creative Commons license, or for public domain use. You're sure to find something that can be used in your project!

Links

audacity.sourceforge.net

Audio Downloads

For a collection of free sound effects you can use in any project, visit:
stopmotionexplosion.com/downloads

Chapter 12

Video Editing

35mm film. Be happy you aren't cutting and pasting this together!

 his chapter answers two frequently asked questions: "How do I put my video clips together?" and "How do I add sound to my movie?"

First, you'll learn some concepts and rules that every video editor should know. Then you'll have an opportunity to practice these rules, as you edit your first movie with a simple video editor.

Combining video clips, dialog, sound effects and music into a finished movie is the last step in the creative process. You'll need to acquire some video editing software first. Fortunately there are two great options.

iMovie

OS X (Mac) only. This program can be downloaded from the App Store. The simple interface hides many powerful features, such as greenscreening and audio effects. It also integrates seamlessly with Apple's GarageBand and iPhoto software.

Video Tutorial: Editing in iMovie

Due to space limitations, I have not included an iMovie tutorial in this book. Instead, you can watch a complete video tutorial on the Stopmotion Explosion website.

stopmotionexplosion.com/imovie

Windows Movie Maker

Windows Movie Maker (WMM) is an easy to use video editor packaged with all installations of Windows XP, and Windows Vista. It does not automatically come installed on Windows 7 and versions following; however it can still be downloaded for free.

There are a few different versions of WMM. Windows 7 users can download the **Windows Live** version as part of the Windows Live package; however the Live version lacks many great features, and is more buggy and slower than proceeding versions! Avoid it if possible.

Instead, install **Windows Movie Maker 2.6** (if you are running Windows XP) or **Windows Movie Maker 6.0** (if you are running Vista or later versions)

CHECK IT OUT!

Download the sources for a complete film, *Jack Spelt and the Sandstone Caves* at:

stopmotionexplosion.com/downloads

The easiest way to find these older, better versions of WMM is by googling **"Download Windows Movie Maker 2.6"** or **"Download Windows Movie Maker 6.0".** I've also linked to installers on the Stopmotion Explosion website's download page.

Other Programs

You can spend hundreds to thousands of dollars on video editing software. **Adobe Premiere** is a popular video editor for Windows. Students with a valid ID, or homeschool organization membership can take advantage of Adobe's generous student discounts. Adobe's student license allows commercial work to be done with the software, useful if a day comes when you start getting paid to make movies.

The cheaper **Adobe Premiere Elements** is another option, though its features are limited.

Apple's **Final Cut** editor is available on the App Store, and contains many more features than iMovie.

Sony Vegas is another popular choice. Vegas comes in several flavors, each with different features and prices.

What is Editing?

Editing used to be a hands-on process. Real film was cut and glued (or "spliced") on an editing table and played back with special machines.

This changed when computers became powerful enough to edit video. Instead of gluing strips of film together, modern video editors work with a computer program that assembles media files into a movie. These programs are called Non-Linear Editors, often abbreviated as NLE.

Many of the terms used in a computer-based editing process are taken

Working with 35mm film on an editing table back in the good old days, when editors were rockin' lab coats like mad scientists.

from terms used by film editors. "Cuts" are literal scissor cuts used to remove "clips," short sections of the film roll. These clips were placed in a "bin" with other clips. Sometimes you hear a reference to a piece of footage or an idea ending up on the "cutting room floor," referring to a clip being tossed aside, swept up by the janitor and discarded.

When you sit down and prepare to edit, you are building on previous work. You have written a story, captured footage, recorded dialog, and most importantly, have a vision for the final result.

Edward Dmytryk, (1908-1999) wrote a book titled: *On Film Editing*. In his book he lists seven rules, six of which are still relevant for today's editors.

GLOSSARY

Editing Terms

NLE: Short for Non Linear Editor. Windows Movie Maker is one example.

Sources: Any file used in a movie project. Source files can be audio, video, pictures and graphics.

Project Files: Used by all NLE programs, sound programs and some animation programs. It's a file on the computer that links to your source files and remembers the order they appear in the movie.

Cuts: A term borrowed from film editing. A cut is where two separate pieces of film join, or two video files are divided and brought together.

Scenes: You can think of these as "chapters" in your movie's story. A scene can be made of many individual shots and camera angles, or just one.

Rule 1: Never make a cut without a positive reason

If a shot captures emotion and action well, why show another? Cut only when absolutely necessary.

This rule does not imply that cuts are a bad thing. A cut is just another way to tell your story, and should be used strategically.

Rule 2: When undecided about the exact frame to cut on, cut long rather than short

This rule borrows from a carpentry principle. It's easier to saw boards long and trim them down, than too short and have to tack wood on the end. Cutting a strip of film too short requires gluing the film back together to find a better frame.

You don't have this problem when editing digital video. You can always click "Undo" and restore your work. So, this rule is not relevant for editors today.

Rule 3: Whenever possible cut 'in movement'

If a character's head is turning to look at something, cut to what they see in the middle of the turn. If someone jumps over a log, cut while they're flying through the air. Following this rule will make your cuts invisible to the viewer.

Rule 4: The 'fresh' is preferable to the 'stale'

If you display content that repeats established facts, or doesn't develop the story, your audience's attention will wander. They'll start noticing fingers creeping into the picture, or tape holding the set down. Keep things "fresh" with material that advances the story.

This rule is related to the third rule. Dead space between cuts will distract your audience, giving them time to concentrate on unimportant details.

Rule 5: All scenes should begin and end with continuing action

If a scene begins with a boy pulling the cord of a lawnmower, the scene should end as he finishes mowing and reaches for the weedwhacker. He has successfully completed one action and is moving to the next.

Scenes should begin with action, and finish with the start of another action.

Rule 6: Cut for proper values rather than proper 'matches'

Continuity is the discipline of matching details between shots in a film. Since shots are usually filmed out-of-order, there's a high possibility of discrepancies between them.

For example, if a character drinks a glass of water, sets the empty glass down, and the next shot shows the same glass full of water, continuity is broken. This will confuse the audience.

Keeping continuity is not high on the editor's to-do list. These issues should be resolved during filming. If two shots don't match, you can try editing around it... but if you must choose between a poor shot with bad continuity, and a great shot with bad continuity, choose the great shot. Spielberg does so, you should too.

Rule 7: Substance first, then form

Dmytryk believed the editor's primary concern was improving the emotional power of the film's story, not following rules or set patterns Editing is not a technical exercise, like math or science, but an art.

One of the best ways to learn the art of editing is by watching the work others have done, and asking questions about it. Why was the movie cut like this? What was the creator's intent? How could I apply these techniques in my work?

Editing Basics

This chapter will teach you basic NLE technique using **Windows Movie Maker 6.0**. Though this program lacks features that high-end editing programs have, it's a great way to start learning basic skills that can be applied in any editing program you use.

If you're on a Mac, then watch the **iMovie** video tutorial linked to at the beginning of this chapter.

Organization

Organizing resources you've gathered during the planning and shooting of your movie is important. You'll be more productive if you can find everything when it's needed!

Your resources might include animated video clips, photos, dialog you've recorded, sound effects, music, etc...

Give source files descriptive names, so you can find them later. Make new folders for each project and back up the folder frequently. It hurts to lose hours of hard work!

You'll also need a good collection of sound effects. If you arrange them in folders by subject, you'll have a valuable resource for your projects. Many free sounds can be found on the Internet or recorded yourself. Higher quality sounds can be purchased and downloaded.

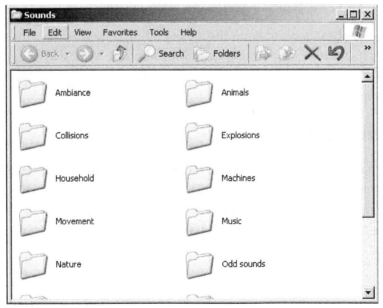

A well stocked and organized sound collection.

Introduction to Windows Movie Maker

As you learn the features of Windows Movie Maker and start working with the program, remember two things:

 Most actions can be undone by clicking *Edit > Undo*. Remember this when you make a mistake!

2 If you have a problem or question that's not answered here, tap into the community of WMM users on the Internet. Type "Windows Movie Maker" into any search engine, and a wealth of information will appear. Add a few words related to your problem or a description of the error message (if any) to narrow down the results.

Let's begin! If you need to install Windows Movie Maker, you can follow the links on the Stopmotion Explosion website's Downloads page, or find an installer on Google.

Start Windows Movie Maker (referred to as **WMM** from here on). It's usually found in the Windows Program Menu. If you cannot find the program, run a search for it.

To make WMM look like the illustration on page 203, click *View > Timeline*, then display the Collections by clicking *View> Collections*. Up in the top left corner, click *File*, then *New Project*.

Video Tutorial: Editing in Movie Maker

Watch a complete Windows Movie Maker video tutorial on the StopmotionExplosion.com website!

stopmotionexplosion.com/wmm

Clip Collection

This part of an NLE goes by many names, depending on the program you are using. "Clip Collection," "Clip Panel," and "Browser" are a few. The collection is where source files are placed before they are used in the project. It's like a box for your files, holding them until they are dragged onto the timeline for editing.

The Clip Collection

The work of moving sources into the Collection is called "Importing." Importing is the first step to creating a movie in an NLE. Let's import a few sources right now!

Click **Tools** at the top of the screen, then, in the drop-down menu that appears, click **New Collection Folder**. Name the folder something relevant by going to the top of the screen, clicking **Edit**, then **Rename**. Great! We're all set to import some sources.

Video Tutorial: Edit in High Definition (HD)

With a few extra steps, it's possible to edit and save HD video from Windows Movie Maker! To learn how this is done, visit: *stopmotionexplosion.com/wmm-hd*

Windows Movie Maker shortly after launching

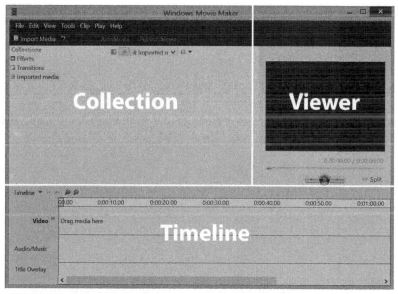

The three main areas of Windows Movie Maker. In this screenshot I've labeled them "Clip Collection," "Viewer," and "Timeline."

Importing Video

In Windows Movie Maker, you import files by clicking *File* in the upper left corner, then *Import into Collections...* or *Import Media Items*. A file dialog comes up.

Navigate around the computer until you find one of your video files. Click the file to select it, then hit the *Import* button. If you have many

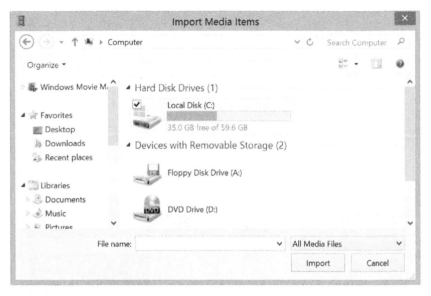

video files to import, you can select several at once, by holding the *Ctrl* key down and clicking each file. When finished, click *Import*.

If you're using the older WMM 2.6, after importing a bunch of video sources, you have a collection folder for every imported clip.

It's better to have all the clips in one folder. Fortunately, you can drag the movie sources out of their individual folders, into the one we created earlier.

Once you've done this, you can just delete the empty folders. Click them and hit *Delete* on your keyboard, or up at the top of the screen, click *Edit > Delete*.

Collection: nextdayoutsidehouse Drag a clip and drop it on the timeline below.				
Name	Duration	Start...	End Time	Dimensio
nextdayoutsidehouse	0:00:06	0:00:00	0:00:06	640 x 48

Collections
- Video Effects
- Video Transitions
- Collections
  - grandpaandjacktalk1
  - grandpaandjacktalk2
  - grandpaandjacktalk3
  - grandpaandjacktalk4
  - grandpaandjacktalk5
  - grandpaandjacktalk6
  - Jack Spelt
  - johnnyenterscave
  - knightleavescave
  - nextdayoutsidehouse
  - oldmaninoffice
  - piratesinside1
  - piratesinside2
  - piratesinside3
  - piratesinyard1
  - piratesinyard2

Newly imported sources in individual folders (WMM 2.6)

Collection: Jack Spelt Drag a clip and drop it on the timeline below.				
Name	Duration	Start...	End Time	Dimensio
grandpaandjacktalk1	0:00:09	0:00:00	0:00:09	640 x 48
grandpaandjacktalk2	0:00:03	0:00:00	0:00:03	640 x 48
grandpaandjacktalk3	0:00:14	0:00:00	0:00:14	640 x 48
grandpaandjacktalk4	0:00:07	0:00:00	0:00:07	640 x 48
grandpaandjacktalk5	0:00:07	0:00:00	0:00:07	640 x 48
grandpaandjacktalk6	0:00:14	0:00:00	0:00:14	610 x 48
johnnyenterscave	0:00:12	0:00:00	0:00:12	640 x 48
knightleavescave	0:00:04	0:00:00	0:00:04	640 x 48
nextdayoutsidehouse	0:00:06	0:00:00	0:00:06	640 x 48
oldmaninoffice	0:00:24	0:00:00	0:00:24	640 x 48
piratesinside1	0:00:06	0:00:00	0:00:06	640 x 48
piratesinside2	0:00:11	0:00:00	0:00:11	640 x 48
piratesinside3	0:00:21	0:00:00	0:00:21	640 x 48
piratesinyard1	0:00:21	0:00:00	0:00:21	610 x 48
piratesinyard2	0:00:02	0:00:00	0:00:02	640 x 48

Collections
- Video Effects
- Video Transitions
- Collections
  - grandpaandjacktalk2
  - grandpaandjacktalk3
  - grandpaandjacktalk4
  - grandpaandjacktalk5
  - grandpaandjacktalk6
  - Jack Spelt
  - johnnyenterscave
  - knightleavescave
  - nextdayoutsidehouse
  - oldmaninoffice
  - piratesinside1
  - piratesinside2
  - piratesinside3
  - piratesinyard1
  - piratesinyard2

All the sources moved into one folder. Delete empty folders (WMM 2.6)

Importing Sound

Let's import some sound files. Click on the movie's collection folder and again, click: *File > Import...* Navigate to your sound folder and start importing every sound you think the film will require. Car sounds, people sounds, water sounds, explosions, anything.

Missing Sources

Importing is only *telling* the NLE where source files are on your computer. Sources are *not moved or copied*, only linked to, or referenced. If you move or delete sources on the hard drive, the missing source files will look like little red X's in the viewer:

205

Name	Duration	Start...	End Time	Dimens
Clip (4)	0:00:14	0:00:00	0:00:14	640 x 4
Clip (5)	0:00:03	0:00:00	0:00:03	640 x 4

Lost source files!

Double-clicking a missing source brings up a file dialog, allowing you to locate the original file, which hopefully has been moved, and NOT deleted! If it's gone you'll need your backup. You have a backup, right?

More Organization

Earlier in the chapter I mentioned how important organization is. Looking at this screenshot, you can see how I've arranged the video and audio sources in separate folders.

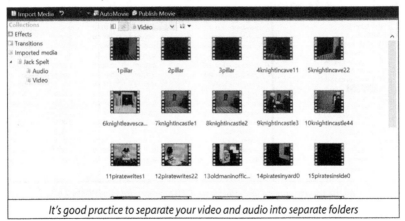

It's good practice to separate your video and audio into separate folders

You can make these "folders-within-folders" by right-clicking the movie's collection folder, and selecting "New Collection Folder"

You've done a lot of work! It's time to save the project. Click *File > Save Project*, and give the project a name. Then click the *Save* button. Save

Backing up your work!

You should back up the project file too, along with your sources. By doing so, you can re-construct your movie if anything happens. Windows Movie Maker project files have the **.mswmm** extension.

frequently! If the unthinkable happens, you'll feel much better if you've only lost 5 minutes of work.

Timeline

The timeline looks a little like a ruler, except it measures time instead of inches. First, notice how the timeline is divided by several horizontal lines. These spaces are called "tracks." If you look on the left side, you'll

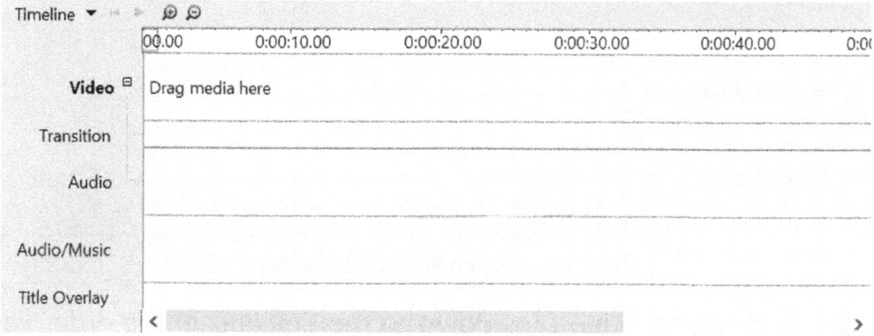

The Timeline!

see each track is labeled. There's a "Video" track with two subtracks: "Audio" and "Transition". There's also an "Audio" track, and a "Title Overlay" track. (Click the plus icon if you don't see all these tracks).

Not surprisingly, video sources are placed on the "Video" track, and audio sources on the "Audio" track.

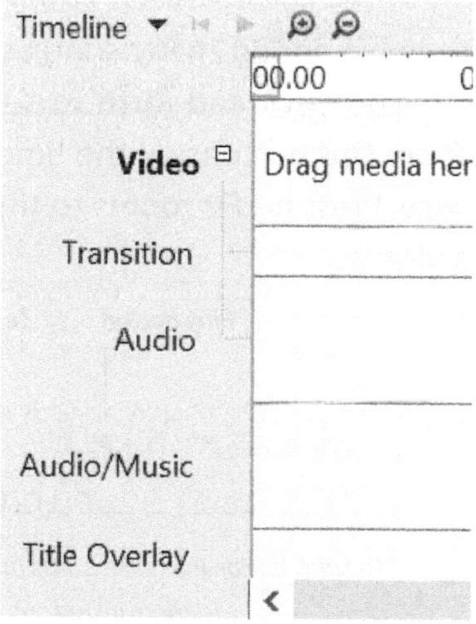

Adding Video to the Timeline

We're ready to start putting the movie together! Go into the Collection folder and find the video source that appears first in your movie. Click and drag it down to the "Video" track. See how the cursor changes when you're over the timeline? Release the mouse button to place the first source.

207

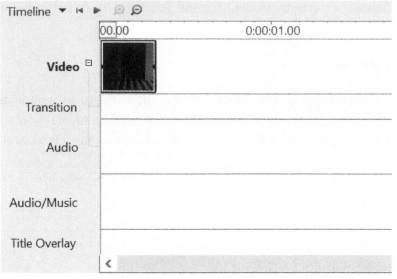

First video source added to the timeline.

Continue dragging video clips down to the timeline, in the order you want them to appear. Now play everything by clicking the *Play* button on the timeline

If you've followed these instructions correctly, your video clips should play back in perfect order in the Viewer. Congratulations! You've taken another step towards completing your movie!

If you've added many sources to the timeline, you'll soon get tired of scrolling back and forth to see them all. By clicking the *Zoom In* and *Zoom Out* buttons on the timeline, you can see more of the timeline at once. Pressing *F9* zooms to the point where everything in the timeline is visible.

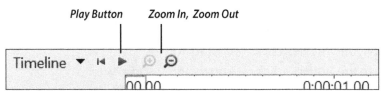

*The play button looks like a little arrow pointing right. The rewind button is next to it.
To zoom in and out, click the magnifying glass buttons.*

To the left of *Zoom In* and *Zoom Out* are two buttons that play and rewind the timeline. You've already clicked *Play.* Click the left-pointing arrow to rewind the timeline.

Adding Audio to the Timeline

Now that the movie has some video, it's time to add sound. Audio sources are added to the timeline exactly like video sources.

Look in the Collection folder, and find the first sound you want in the movie. Drag it down onto the "Audio" track in the timeline.

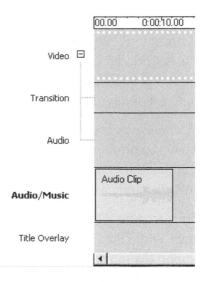

A source added to the audio track

You probably noticed you couldn't drag the sound onto the first audio track, only the one underneath it. The first track is for audio contained in video clips. After you've placed a few more audio clips on the timeline, you'll find yourself wishing for another track of audio. I'll explain a workaround for this. For now, press the *Play* button.

HEADS UP

Troubleshooting

If the video does not play back smoothly, but stutters and jerks, skipping frames and sections of video, this can be a symptom of not compressing your video before editing.

Page to the **Frame Conversion** chapter at the end of this book for video compression instructions.

The movie will play, and you will hear the sound! Chances are the sound is not in the right place. Stop and rewind the movie, then click and drag the sound clip along the track, until it's roughly where you want it. Continue playing and tweaking the sound's position, until it's exactly where it needs to be.

WMM allows sounds to be "stacked." They may be stacked two high, by dragging them on top of each other. This is not a perfect solution because the sounds fade in and out, but if you have several short sounds, this is a handy way to blend them together.

To overcome WMM's one audio track limitation, you can fill the audio track with clips, export the entire movie using a high-quality setting, import the movie back into WMM and continue adding sounds. I explain the export process on page 224.

0:00:05.80 / 0:00:07.67

Split

The Viewer

Let's discuss the Viewer next, before editing the rest of our movie. The viewer and timeline work closely together. It's hard to use one without knowing how the other works.

Viewer

The viewer is like a TV screen with a DVD player attached. The movie project you're editing is the DVD. You can play the project by clicking the play button. You stop playback by clicking stop, and pause the project by clicking pause. It's important to understand that when you play, pause, rewind or fast forward, you're moving through *time*.

In the viewer, click the play button again. Notice two things. First, in the viewer, two times are displayed. The time on the left shows how much time the sources in the project add up to, the *length* of the project. This could be anywhere from no time at all, up to 4 hours. Current time is displayed on the right. The current time is where the playhead rests on the timeline.

Click the **Play** button once more. This time, look at the timeline. See that vertical line moving along?

This is the playhead. It marks the current playing time, and can be used for many other things. Try this!

Move the mouse to the top of the timeline, so the cursor rests over the ruler measuring time. A vertical line will appear under the cursor, with a little box next to it, showing what time you're pointing at. Move the cursor back and forth. See the time change?

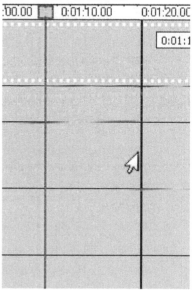

The black bar displays the "time" you're pointing at.

Move the cursor along the "ruler" somewhere in the middle of the sources you've placed, and click the mouse.

The playhead jumps to the time you clicked. Look at the viewer. You've advanced to the middle of the movie, without touching fast-forward or rewind! Now, try clicking the little square on the top of the playhead, and dragging it along the ruler (watch the viewer as you do this).

You are rewinding and fast forwarding through the movie by dragging the playhead around. This technique is called "scrubbing," and is very handy for quickly moving to a place in the project.

You might be tempted to do all of your rewinding and fast forwarding this way, but the playback buttons in the viewer are useful too. In particular, the *Previous Frame* and *Next Frame* buttons let you move the playhead very precisely, one frame at a time.

Look at this picture for a quick reference for the buttons in the viewer.

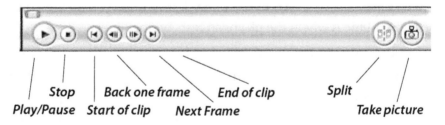

These buttons work somewhat like the controls on a DVD player remote. Depending on your version of WMM, not all of the buttons pictured may be visible.

- *PLAY*: Starts playing the movie from the playhead's position (changes to PAUSE when clicked). Hitting the space bar also plays and pauses your movie.
- *STOP*: Stops playback, and rewinds (moves playhead) to the beginning of the project.
- *BACK*: Moves playhead to beginning of clip.
- *PREVIOUS FRAME*: Rewinds one frame. Hold down to rewind.
- *NEXT FRAME*: Moves forward one frame. Hold down to fast-forward.
- *NEXT*: Moves playhead to end of clip (or beginning of next clip).

In addition to these navigational buttons are two with editing functions: *Take Picture*, and *Split Clip*. I'll cover their uses in the next section of this chapter.

All these buttons are also accessible from the *Play* menu. If you are using WMM 6.0, click *Tools* > *Take Picture from Preview* to capture a freeze-frame.

Working with Clips

Let's keep editing the movie. Add any remaining video sources, and a few essential sounds to the timeline. Place sources roughly where they belong.

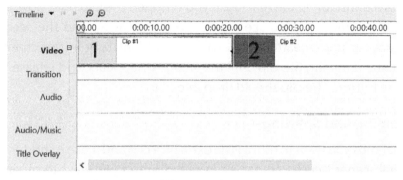

Two clips: Clip #1 and Clip #2 have been added to the timeline

If you accidentally mess up and place a wrong source on the timeline, then click the source, select *Edit* > *Delete*, and try again. Remember, you're not deleting anything on the computer! You're only removing the source from the timeline. Clicking *Edit* > *Undo* is another way to fix the mistake (hit *Ctrl+Z*).

If you want to drop a source between two clips on the timeline, simply drag and drop the source where the two clips meet. If the source is already on the timeline, you can shuffle clips around and arrange them in a different order by dragging and dropping. Don't forget, you can zoom in and out to see more of the timeline.

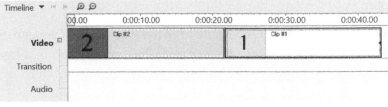

Clip #2 has been dragged and dropped in front of Clip #1

If you try to drag a clip backwards onto another clip, you'll notice a funny blue wedge appearing on the clip that's not moving.

This is a transition in the making. If you dropped the clip right now, and played the movie, you'd see the first clip fade away, and the second one appear underneath it. I'll explain transitions later in this chapter. Continue dragging the clip until the wedge disappears, and release the mouse button. The clip should drop into place.

Trimming and Splitting

Sometimes you want to trim a little extra off a clip and make it shorter. Or, several scenes may be contained in one clip, and you want to separate them. This is where trimming and splitting are very handy.

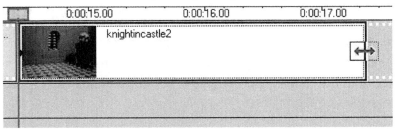

This clip needs to be shortened

First, select the clip by clicking. Move the mouse to one end of the clip.

You'll see the mouse cursor change into a box with two arrows. Click and drag the mouse towards the beginning of the clip to trim the clip down to size.

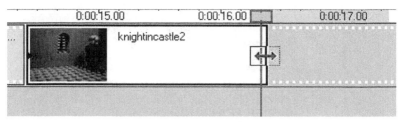

Removing about 3/4 second from the clip

If you trim the clip too short, you can drag it back to its full length.

While you're dragging the end of the clip, the viewer shows what frame you're trimming to. To trim in smaller increments, zoom in on the clip.

Splitting

Cuts are typically made by chopping, or "splitting" a source into smaller clips. You split a source into pieces, and insert clips between them.

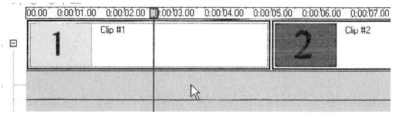

Preparing to split a clip

Move the playhead where you want the split to occur. Don't forget: the viewer's *Next Frame* and *Previous Frame* buttons let you move the playhead one frame at a time. Once the playhead is sitting on the frame where you want the split to happen, click the *Split* button in the viewer.

The Split button

Snip! The source has been split into two parts.

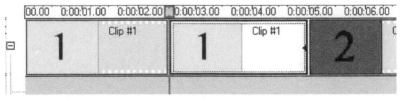

Clip split!

Each half is an individual clip. The clips can be moved, trimmed, and split again if you wish.

Copying and Pasting

Clips can be copied, cut, and pasted, just like you were working with text. Select a clip by clicking, and go to *Edit > Copy.*

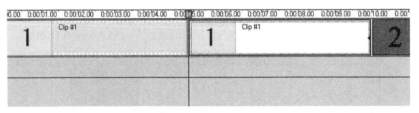

Clip #1 has been copied and pasted

Clips are pasted at the playhead, so before you paste, drag the playhead where you want the clip, and click *Edit > Paste.*

Storyboard

This is a different way to arrange video sources on the timeline. It's not as powerful as the timeline method, but it's simple, and a great way to throw sources together in a hurry. Click *View > Storyboard.*

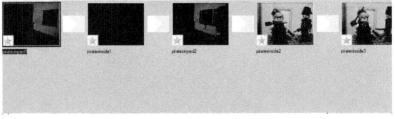

The Storyboard view

This is the "storyboard" layout of WMM. It's pretty straightforward. Video and pictures are dragged and dropped onto the big squares. You can shuffle sources around by dragging and dropping them between squares.

Storyboard view is a handy way to add and edit video **transitions** and **effects**.

Transitions

A transition is an artistic, visual way to move between two clips. A transition can be used to show the passage of time, to soften an abrupt cut, or show a change in location.

The most common and flexible transition is the **Dissolve**. Sometimes Dissolve is called a "Crossfade," or "Mix." WMM calls the dissolve a "Fade" (it's confusing, because there's an incorrectly labeled Dissolve in the collection. It's not the same thing). Another commonly used transition is the **Wipe**, in which a line or shape makes a moving boundary between two clips.

Everything else falls into the effect transitions category. Effect transitions can look like anything; from pages turning to newspapers flying or fancy 3D shatter effects. WMM comes with a large selection, which you can preview by clicking *Transitions* in the Collections folder.

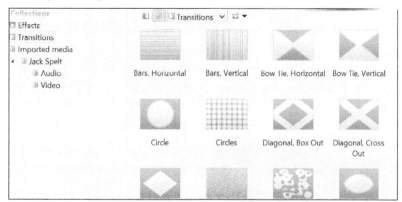

Bars, Bowties and Circles

Clicking a transition loads a preview into the viewer, which you can play to see what it looks like.

Adding a transition is simple. In the timeline, pick a video source, and start dragging it backwards, on top of the one before it.

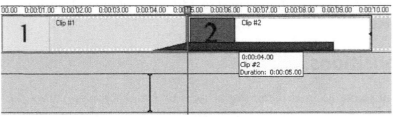

Transition in the making

A blue wedge begins forming, and a box appears next to the cursor, showing how far the clip has been dragged. Release the clip after it has moved back about a second.

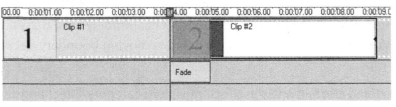

Cross fade transition completed

Hit **Play** to see the transition. The first clip "dissolves," and the second appears underneath it.

You'll notice a box labeled "Fade" has appeared. This is a Transition track. The box is labeled "Fade," because this is the kind of transition being used. Remember the transitions we were looking at earlier? By dragging and dropping transitions on this box, the type of transition can be changed. Try it!

It may be tempting to fill a movie with wacky transitions, but it's more cinematic to use only cuts, dissolves and wipes.

Save effect transitions for used car commercials.

It's simpler to add transitions in the storyboard view, and fine-tune them in the timeline. To add transitions in the storyboard, simply drag and drop them on top of the smaller boxes. A 1.25 second transition will be added between the clips. (*1.25* seconds is the default length. This can be changed under *Tools > Options*.)

Transitions are removed the same way sources are. Select and delete them.

Effects

Return to the timeline view (if you haven't already), go to the Collections folder, and click *Effects*.

Many interesting effects appear. All of them can be previewed in the viewer by double-clicking.

Choose an interesting effect. Drag and drop it on top of a clip in the timeline. (You do the same thing in storyboard view; simply drag and drop an effect onto a video square).

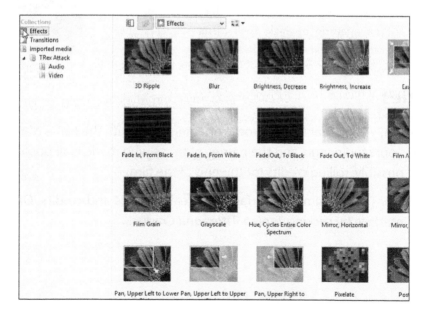

A star appears on the clip. This shows an effect has been applied. Play the movie to see the result of your effect.

Several effects are particularly useful, including Fade In/Fade Out, Ease

in/Ease Out, and different options for flipping the movie's picture around. Making your video look "old" is fun.

If you apply several effects to a clip, chances are you'll want to remove some. By right-clicking the clip and selecting **Video Effects...** you can remove some of, or all of, the effects.

The star indicates that this clip has an effect applied to it.

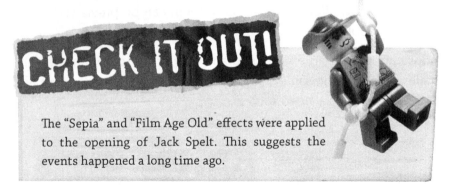

CHECK IT OUT!

The "Sepia" and "Film Age Old" effects were applied to the opening of Jack Spelt. This suggests the events happened a long time ago.

Titles

Eventually you'll want to add some opening titles, with the name of your film, your studio logo, and the names of those who made it all possible. And possibly, rolling credits for the end of the film.

WMM has a very simple interface for creating titles and credits. Open this interface by clicking **Tools > Titles and Credits...**

Click **Title at the beginning.**

There's two areas for type. The top box is for the main title. Any text added here is displayed in big bold letters. The bottom box is for a smaller sub-title.

Type something like: **"My Amazing Movie"** in the top box, and **"It's the Best!"** in the bottom. Look at the viewer.

Where do you want to add a title?

Title at the beginning

Title before the selected clip

Title on the selected clip

Credits at the end

Cancel

Title and Credits tool

The text is displayed in the viewer as you type. After you finish, the text is automatically animated.

WMM comes with many different title animations, and allows you to change the color and type of text. These options can be accessed by clicking **Change the title animation**, and **Change the text font and color.**

When you're finished, click **Add title**, and a new title clip appears on the timeline!

A new title. Click the play button to see it fade in and out.

Adding credits is done the same way, except there are more fields to fill in. Click **Tools > Titles and Credits...** then **Credits at the end**. Once you're finished, you can change the color and animation by clicking **Change the title animation**, and **Change the text font and color.**

Enter text for title

|

More options:
Change the title animation
Change the text font and color

Credits. Add names on the lines.

After titles and credits have been placed on the timeline, they can be adjusted to any length you desire. Using the previously described method for trimming, click and drag the title clip's ends. When you play the clip again, you'll notice the titles are moving a lot slower, or a lot faster, depending whether you made the clip longer or shorter.

The shorter your film is, the shorter your titles should be. I have come to dislike credits at the end of YouTube shorts, (but that didn't stop me from adding them when I first started making movies!)

CHECK IT OUT!

A title *"Many years later..."* was placed between the pirate writing a letter, and the old man looking at the map. You can use a title to set the time and place, like, *"Paris 1789."*

Recording Sound and Dialog

WMM includes a handy sound recording tool. It's useful for recording character dialog, because the video plays while you record, and the recorded clip is placed directly on the timeline. Open the recorder window by clicking *Tools > Narrate Timeline...*

This is another simple interface that needs very little explanation. Click *Start Narration* to begin recording sound. When you're finished, click *Stop Narration*. A save file dialog will pop up. Name the sound and save the file. It will automatically be imported and placed on the timeline, at the playhead's current position.

Note that he playhead must be moved to a point in the timeline where there's no sound, or the record button will be grayed out. If you click *"Show Options"*, you can select the microphone source.

> Narrate Timeline
>
> Start Narration   Input level:
>
> Stop Narration
>
> Close
>
> How do I add narration?
>
> Show options

Photos and Stills

Take Picture

You can take a single frame from your movie and use it as you would a video source. In WMM, these still frames are made by clicking the picture button located in the viewer (WMM 2.6), or clicking *Tools > Take Picture from Preview.* (WMM 6.0) After you save this "picture" (frame), WMM will automatically import it into the Clip Collection. Frames are kept in the collection folder until placed on the timeline.

If used carefully, this technique can produce great results. Additionally, you can take still pictures with a digital camera and insert them in the timeline like a video file.

Sharing Your Movie!

It's time to package the project into a movie file that can be shared with the world! In WMM, the process begins by clicking *File* > *Save Movie File...* or *Publish Movie...* Then click *...Computer*, then *Next*.

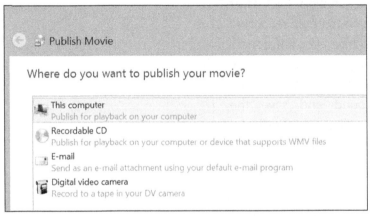

A window appears. Choose a name for the movie file, and decide where it will be saved on the computer. You should make a special folder for your finished movies, but if you're in a hurry, it's OK to save them on your desktop. Type a name for your movie file and click *Next*.

Tweaking settings to achieve the best picture with the smallest file size is a fine art! You could go with what the wizard has suggested–a relatively small, low quality movie, or underneath *More Settings,* many different options appear. The "VHS Quality" option is a good choice for standard definition 640 x 480 video.

It's a good idea to export your movie with the best possible quality settings, especially if you're uploading the video to a sharing site, like

YouTube. The website will re-encode the video, so it's best to upload high-quality material.

Publish Movie

Choose the settings for your movie

The setting you select determines the quality and file size of your movie:

○ Best quality for playback on <u>m</u>y computer (recommended)

○ <u>C</u>ompress to: 510 ⌃⌄ KB ⌄

● More <u>s</u>ettings: Windows Media VHS Quality (1.0 Mbps) ⌄

DV-AVI (NTSC)
Windows Media Portable Device (1.0 Mbps)
Windows Media DVD Quality (3.0 Mbps)
Windows Media DVD Widescreen Quality (3.0 Mbps)
Windows Media Low Bandwidth (117 kbps)
Windows Media VHS Quality (1.0 Mbps)
Windows Media HD 1280x720
Windows Media HD 1440x1080
Windows Media HD 1920x1080
Windows Media HD 960x720

Movie settings

File type: Windows Media Video (WMV)

Bit rate: 1.0 Mbps

Display size: 640 x 480 pixels

Aspect ratio: 4:3

Frames per second: 30

Estimated space required:
1051 KB

Estimated disk space available on drive C:
33.46 GB

After clicking **Publish**, the movie will begin exporting. Depending on the length of the movie and your computer's processing power, it may take a few minutes. You could jump around the room impatiently waiting for the export to finish, or you could check out some of these additional resources online!

Video Tutorial: Exporting HD Video

To export HD quality video from WMM as pictured, refer to the instructions at: *stopmotionexplosion.com/wmm-hd*

Movie Maker Resources

A thriving Internet community has sprung up around Windows Movie Maker. Here are two websites you should visit. Both contain a wealth of information about the program!

www.papajohn.org

www.windowsmoviemakers.net

More Effects

Eventually you may become bored with the effects, transitions, and titles that WMM is packaged with. The Pixelan company has created a wide variety of effects and transitions for WMM. They are available in downloadable packs for a moderate price. Multiple packs can be purchased for additional savings:

www.pixelan.com

Many effects come free! The Windows Movie Makers forum has an entire section devoted to custom effects, transitions, and titles:

www.windowsmoviemakers.net/forums

www.thefxarchive.com

Links

Adobe Software
www.adobe.com

Final Cut
www.apple.com/finalcutstudio

www.apple.com/finalcutexpress

Sony Vegas
www.sonycreativesoftware.com/vegassoftware

Movie Maker Shortcuts

Following is a list of common WMM tasks, and keyboard shortcuts for each. Learn how to edit with one hand on the mouse, the other on your keyboard. You'll work faster, and more efficiently.

Function   Shortcut

Open project . . . . *CTRL+O*

Save project. . . . . *CTRL+S*

Export movie . . . . *CTRL+P*

Capture live video from camera . . . . *CTRL+R*

Import source file . . . . *CTRL+I*

Undo last action . . . . *CTRL+Z*

Redo last action . . . . *CTRL+Y*

Cut. . . . . *CTRL+X*

Copy . . . . *CTRL+C*

Paste . . . . *CTRL+V*

Delete. . . . . *DELETE*

Select all clips . . . . *CTRL+A*

Rename collection or clip *F2*

Clear the timeline . . . . *CTRL+DELETE*

Switch storyboard/timeline view. . . . . *CTRL+T*

Zoom in on the timeline . . . . *PAGE DOWN*

Zoom out on the timeline . . . . *PAGE UP*

Add selected clips to the timeline . . . . *CTRL+D*

Preview project in full screen . . . . *ALT+ENTER*

Set start trim point. . . . . *CTRL+SHIFT+I*

Set end trim point . . . . *CTRL+SHIFT+O*

Clear trim points . . . . *CTRL+SHIFT+DELETE*

Split a clip . . . . *CTRL+L*

Combine contiguous clips . . . . *CTRL+M*

Nudge clip left . . . . *CTRL+SHIFT+B*

Nudge clip right . . . . *CTRL+SHIFT+N*

Play and Pause . . . .*SPACE*

Playhead Right . . . . *ALT+RIGHT ARROW*

Playhead Left . . . . *ALT+LEFT ARROW*

Chapter 13

Files and Formats

 So far, we've created basic movies and saved them to the computer. Occasionally I've mentioned compressing movies with software called a codec that makes your movies easier to play and share.

There are three concepts to understand: container formats, image compression, and codecs.

Container Formats

Container formats are computer files, a type of computer "package." All kinds of containers exist. Filmmakers constantly use container formats holding video, images, and sounds.

If you have made animations with **SME**, you have used the **AVI** or **MP4** containers. These are common video containers. Both can hold one track of video, and two tracks of audio.

You've also used the **JPG**, **PNG,** or **BMP** container. These containers hold still images.

If you've done some editing and added sound effects to a movie, you were probably working with **WAV** files, a common sound container.

Container formats are almost always referred to as "files." You will see references to "JPG files," "AVI files," "WAV files" and so on.

File Extensions

All files on the computer have an extension as part of their file name. When the computer looks at an extension, it knows what program should open the file. Extensions always come after the file name.

- The file "Videoplayer.exe" has a **.exe** extension (it's a computer program).
- "Clip01.avi" has an **.avi** extension (it's a video file).
- "MyTextDocument.txt" has a **.txt** extension (it's a text file).

Extensions are usually invisible until you turn them on through your computer settings.

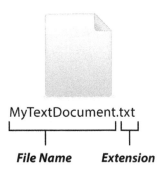

MyTextDocument.txt

File Name   *Extension*

Windows Extensions

On Windows computers, open your computer's Control Panel from the Start Menu, search for *Folder Options*, click the *View* tab, and uncheck *Hide extensions for known file types*. Click *OK*.

Mac Extensions

In OS X, click *Finder > Preferences* and under *Advanced*, check *Show all file extensions*.

Compression

When you make a movie with SME and set the codec settings to *Raw Video (Uncompressed)*, the video is saved in an AVI container in a complete, unmodified state. The file contains the exact data captured.

The contents of a container format may be "compressed," and made smaller with the help of math formulas.

How does this work? Here's an example.

Say we have some footage of the clear blue sky. The uncompressed footage contains data for every point of color in the sky. Since the sky is blue, there are a lot of blue pixels with identical information in every frame. This duplicated information makes the video file larger.

A compressed version of this footage will contain numbers specifying the color of blue, and the size and location of the area that it covers, instead of duplicating the blue pixels over and over in each frame. These formulas are much smaller than the pixels they replace, making the video file smaller.

Compression formulas can be applied to video, sounds, and still images. A good compression formula can keep sound and video at near-uncompressed quality.

Codecs

Video and audio is compressed (or encoded) with something called a codec. The word "codec" is an acronym. It stands for:

COmpressor-DECompressor: **CODEC**

A codec is used to encode media. It is also used to decode media.

Codecs: Technical Explanation

When applied to a media file, a codec analyzes the content with various formulas, and decides how the file can be made smaller, usually by discarding data.

A process that discards information to make something smaller is described as **lossy** since information is being <u>lost</u>. A codec that does not discard data is described as **lossless**.

- Lossless codecs are used during capture and editing.
- Lossy codecs are used for sharing and distributing.

Lossy compressed video looks blurred and blocky. Lossy audio sounds muddy, fuzzed, and tinny, like talking to someone on the phone. The more a file is compressed, the smaller it becomes, and the greater the loss of quality.

Before   **After**

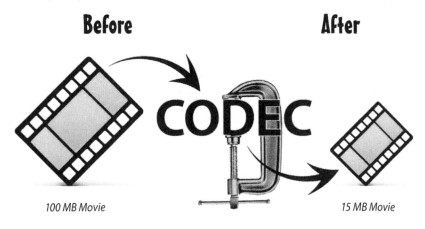

100 MB Movie   *15 MB Movie*

After a media file is compressed with a lossy codec, the original quality is gone. This is why you want to use video compressed with a lossless codec for capturing and editing if possible. Lossy codecs *can* be used for editing, when computer power is limited, or image and sound quality isn't an issue.

Repeatedly compressing video (once during capture, and once after editing) will result in unnecessary loss of quality, because data is discarded twice.

Codecs: TL;DR Explanation

A codec is a program you download, install, and it appears as a compression option in your video software. Computers usually have several dozen codecs installed by default.

Codec List

Codecs can be divided into three groups.

Authoring

Authoring codecs are used during the capture and editing process. They compress the footage very slightly, preserving its original quality. Authoring codecs are also used for archiving purposes (backing your work up.)

Distribution

Distribution codecs are applied before the movie is distributed. The codec is applied during export from the editor, or afterwards; with a separate program.

Legacy

Legacy codecs have been around for a long time. They're found on nearly every computer. Most legacy formats are compatible with Apple, and the QuickTime player. Legacy video, with the exception of MPEG-1, compresses video poorly, with great loss of quality.

You can get away with using MPEG-4 or H.264 for most applications, however you will encounter other codecs, which is why I have listed them for reference.

Compressing for the Web

People are becoming accustomed to high-quality Internet video, and more video sharing sites allow high-definition video uploads. Join the revolution and upload compressed, high resolution movies!

These settings are typical for many video sharing sites. Following a website's recommended procedure for encoding video is the best way to improve the quality of your uploads. Here are some general guidelines.

Video

- **Resolution**: Upload your video with the same resolution it was captured in. This could be 640 x 480, or 320 x 240. YouTube has recently started accepting HD resolution uploads. These should be 1920 x 1080, or 1280 x 720.

- **Frame Rate**: Like your video resolution, this should be left the same as when captured.

- **Codec**: Choose a H.264 or MPEG-4 codec. Other codecs are acceptable, just make sure you have exported the video with the highest quality possible.

- **Video Container**: Currently **MP4**. YouTube and other sites will accept most containers, but if you are trying to get the best video quality possible, use a recommended container format.

Audio

- **Codec**: If possible, choose an MP3 or ACC codec. Most video export dialogs will allow you to choose from a number of codecs. Nearly any will work, but the two above will keep sound quality high, and file size low.

- **Channels**: 2 (stereo audio)

- **Sampling rate**: 44.1kHz

Container Format List

Following is a handy guide to video formats and compression types. Know your extensions!

Type	File	Container Format Description
Audio-Video Interleaved *(Format)*	**.avi**	Universally compatible. Many codec options. Works with any video player as long as the correct codec is installed.
Windows Media Video *(Format & codec. Codec can be applied to .AVI format)*	**.wmv**	WMV was once widely used for Internet video distribution, but is encountered less frequently today. You'll typically see it if you're working with Windows Movie Maker, or other Windows media applications. Great compression! Non-Windows computers may have trouble viewing this format. In these situations, download the open-source **VLC Player.**
QuickTime *(Format & codecs)*	**.mov**	QuickTime is the .AVI format of the Mac world. A large selection of codecs are built into the format. If you are not using OS X, QuickTime Pro, available on the Apple website, can be used for converting files into the QuickTime format.
DV *(Format & codec)*	**.dv**	You're unlikely to see the DV format until you use digital tape-based camcorders. DV is short for Digital Video. The DV codec is applied inside a video camera, as video is being written to tape. This video is transferred from the camcorder to the computer in the .dv format.
DivX *(Format & codec)*	**.divx**	The .divx format is really an .AVI file compressed with the Divx codec. Continue on to the codec section for more information about DivX.

Container Format List continued

Type	File	Container Format Description
MPEG-4 *(Format)*	**.mp4**	MPEG-4 is an advanced video-audio compression algorithm that has its own container format. Most modern codecs and online video use MPEG-4 technology for a high-quality image with a very small file size.
MPEG-1 *(Format)*	**.mpg** **.mpeg**	MPEG-1 has almost become a legacy format, but it has some advantages. Large file sizes, great picture quality. Simple video-to-MPEG converters can be downloaded on the internet.
Flash Video *(Format)*	**.flv**	The Flash Video format usually contains MPEG-4 encoded video. Video uploaded to video sharing websites is often onverted into the FLV format. You can watch FLV video with the open-source **VLC Player**.

Codec Issues

If video is compressed with a codec, moved to another computer, and opened, the video may not play until the correct codec is installed.

Hosting your video on a video sharing site is the best way for viewers to avoid these hassles. You the creator will need to compress and upload the video, which necessitates some knowledge of codecs and video formats.

Quicktime Codecs List

Type	Codec Description
M-JPEG / JPEG *(Authoring)*	If you've ever surfed the web or worked with digital pictures, you've seen a JPEG image. Compresses each frame of video with JPEG compression. Lossless at 100%. No discernible loss at 85%.
PNG *(Authoring)*	Good for compressing RGB video. Lossless. Uses less space than the Animation codec.
None / Raw *(Authoring)*	Uncompressed RGB footage. Will chew through your free hard drive space very quickly.
DV *(Authoring)*	QuickTime can also encode with DV compression! Again, you'll probably use this if you're working with files from a DV camcorder.
Animation *(Authoring)*	Set at 100%, this codec is lossless. Compresses lines of the same color best. (Originally intended for cel-animation, but it works for stop motion too.)
Graphics *(Authoring)*	Intended for lossless compression of 8 bit graphics.
MPEG-4 *(Distribution)*	MPEG-4 is a multimedia standard. Most video sharing sites recommend compressing your video with this codec or the H.264 codec prior to uploading.
H.264 *(Distribution)*	Part of the MPEG-4 standard, this codec is commonly used for encoding and delivering video online.
Sorenson Video 3 *(Legacy)*	Sorenson was a commonly used QuickTime distribution codec. It has since been replaced by H.264 and MPEG-4.

Windows Codecs List

Type	Codec Description
DV *(Authoring)*	I mention DV again, because the DV codec can be applied to AVIs and the QuickTime format. Some programs may allow you to capture to the DV format as you animate.
Windows Media 9 (WM9) *(Distribution)*	The codec used to compress **WMV** video can also be applied to AVI files.*
DivX *(Distribution)*	Back in the day, DivX had associations with movie piracy (arr!) but now enjoys a respected status in the filmmaking community. Download **DivX Free** from **DivX.com**. Download **XviD**, a DivX alternative, from **XviD.org**.
H.261, H.263 *(Legacy)*	Optimized for video conferencing. Works best with video that has little movement. Avoid.
Cinepak codec by Radius *(Legacy)*	Cinepak is probably THE #1 most compatible AVI codec. Plays well on older computers. Encodes very slowly, with poor results. Avoid.

To apply the WMV codec to AVI files, you will need to download the Video Compression Manager application from the Microsoft website. This can be found by googling "wmv9VCMsetup.exe", or searching the Microsoft Downloads center (link on page 239).

Links

Quicktime

www.apple.com/quicktime/download/

Windows Media Video 9 (search for wmv9VCMsetup.exe)

www.microsoft.com/downloads

DivX

www.divx.com/

FLV

en.wikipedia.org/wiki/Flash_Video

VLC Player

www.videolan.org/

Chapter 14

Frame Conversion

There are often times when an animator needs to convert a series of image files into video, and vice-versa.

To give an example; you may have a video file that you would like to add some special effects to with an image editing program. You'll need to break the video apart into individual pictures, add the effect to the images, and convert the images back into video.

Other times, you need to convert a video into a new format, or compress a video file and make it smaller before you start editing.

This can be done easily with the **MPEG Streamclip** application. The program is available for both Windows and OS X, and supports a wide variety of image and video formats. Currently, MPEG Streamclip does not play well with PNG images, so make sure any images you plan to convert into video are already formatted as JPGs or BMPs (i.e. if you're using a frame grabber to capture individual images, make sure you're capturing JPG / BMP images).

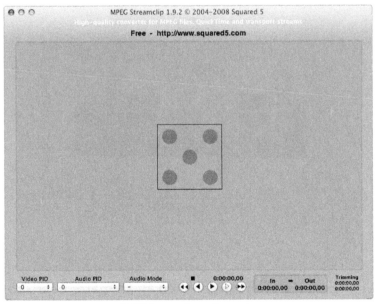

MPEG Streamclip ready to go!

The download link for the program is found at the end of this chapter. The OS X & Windows interface is virtually identical. I captured the screenshots for this tutorial on OS X, but you'll be clicking the same buttons in Windows as you follow along.

If you read the chapter on editing, you'll begin to notice some similarities between MPEG Streamclip and Windows Movie Maker. Files are imported (brought into the program) modified in some way, and exported (output from the program in a new form).

As you'll soon see, MPEG Streamclip has a simple timeline and playhead, the ability to delete single frames, or sections of video, and buttons for playing and previewing your footage. The great thing about the program is its simplicity. Converting a video file can be done in a few clicks!

Video Tutorial: Video Conversion

To watch video tutorials for MPEG Streamclip, visit:

stopmotionexplosion.com/conversion

Compressing a File & Exporting from MPEG Streamclip

Click *File > Open Files...* and navigate through your folders until the movie file you wish to compress appears. Click the file, then click *Open*. For this example, we'll assume this movie is an uncompressed AVI you created in your animation program that you wish to compress before editing.

Bam! The movie file appears in the program window. Click the first small right-facing arrow to play the movie. There are a few additional buttons that allow you to control the speed of the movie as it plays. The left facing arrow will play the frames backwards.

MPEG Streamclip – MPEG-4 Exporter

Compression: H.264   iTunes...

Quality: |||||||||||||||||||||||||||||||||||||||||||||||||||||||||||||||||||||||||||||||||||||||||||| ☐ Multipass
50 %   ☐ B-Frames

☐ Limit Data Rate: Kbps ⬍

Sound: MPEG-4 AAC ⬍   Stereo ⬍   Auto ⬍   256 kbps ⬍

Frame Size: No scaling will be performed   Frame Rate:
◉ 640 × 480 (4:3)   ☐ Frame Blending
○ 854 × 480 (16:9)   ☐ Better Downscaling
○ 640 × 480 (unscaled)
○ 720 × 576 (DV–PAL)   Deselect for progressive movies:
○ 720 × 480 (DV–NTSC)   ☑ Interlaced Scaling
○ 1280 × 720 (HDTV 720p)   ☑ Reinterlace Chroma
○ 1920 × 1080 (HDTV 1080i)
○ Other: 320 ▾ × 240 ▾   ☐ Deinterlace Video

Field Dominance: Upper Field First ⬍   Use "Upper Field First" for all codecs except DV

Rotation: No ⬍

Zoom: 100 ▾ % X/Y   1 ▾   Center   0 ,   0

☐ Cropping: Top 0   Left 0   Bottom 0   Right 0   Destination ⬍

Presets...   Reset All   Adjustments...

Preview   ☐ Fast Start   Cancel   Make MP4

To export a compressed version of the movie, click *File > Export to MPEG-4...* if you're planning to edit the file in iMovie.

Click *Export to AVI...* if you're planning to edit in Windows Movie Maker. This is important, as you'll see in a bit.

If you clicked *Export to MPEG-4*, you'll see the window on the next page. There are a lot of options to click here! First, uncheck the *Interlaced Scaling* box (animations made with webcams and digital cameras aren't interlaced). Then click the *iTunes...* button in the top right corner.

```
┌──────────────────────────────────────────────────┐
│                  MPEG Streamclip                   │
├──────────────────────────────────────────────────┤
│ Please choose a preset for your iPod/iPhone/Apple  │
│ TV:                                                │
│  ○ iPod 640 × 480 (4:3)      Use these presets as a starting
│  ○ iPod 640 × 360 (16:9)     point when you are exporting
│  ○ iPod 320 × 240 (4:3)      for iTunes/iPod/iPhone/Apple
│  ○ iPod 320 × 180 (16:9)     TV.
│  ○ iPhone 432 × 320 (4:3)
│  ○ iPhone 480 × 272 (16:9)
│  ● Apple TV 4:3 (SD)
│  ○ Apple TV 16:9 (SD)
│  ○ Apple TV 960 × 540 (HD)
│  ○ Apple TV 1280 × 720 (HD)
│  ○ 3GP 176 × 144
│                         [ Cancel ]    [    OK    ]
└──────────────────────────────────────────────────┘
```

If your animation was created using a non-HD camera, click the *Apple TV 4:3 (SD)* option, or *16:9* if you were shooting in a widescreen ratio. Otherwise, click one of the HD options (either will work). You can select a 1080 x 1920 resolution on the previous screen, if you need it.

After making your selection, click *OK*. Click *Make MP4*. Save the video file somewhere you will remember.

The file will process. When it's done, you can open it up in iMovie, or the editor of your choice.

Exporting for Windows Movie Maker

If you're compressing a video to edit in Windows Movie Maker, the process is a little different. Click *File > Export to AVI...* then in the top drop-down menu, click *Apple Motion Jpeg A*.

Sound should be set to either *No Sound* or *Uncompressed* in the drop down menu. Set the video resolution by checking one of the options available in the window – again this depends what the resolution of the original file was, and what output you need for editing. Finally, click *Make AVI* and save the file to your computer.

Converting Video into Frames

Instead of exporting a new video file as we did in the previous section, what if you wanted to export a series of images for editing in an image editor?

As previously, open a video file in MPEG Streamclip. Then, click *File > Export to Other Formats*. In the top drop-down menu, click *Image Sequence*. Click the *Options* button on the right. This window should appear.

```
Export Image Sequence Settings

Format:    [ JPEG                    ▲▼]

Frames per second:  [      ] [▲▼]

☑ Insert space before number

[ Options... ]      [ Cancel ]   [  OK  ]
```

Choose *JPEG* as the format, and select the correct frames per second (i.e. 15 FPS, if this is the speed of the animation). Click *OK*. Then, in the previous window, click *OK* again. You'll be asked where you want to save the images. MAKE A FOLDER FOR THEM, because you're creating a LOT of image files very quickly. When MPEG Streamclip finishes, you'll be ready to start editing!

Converting Frames into Video

This is the section to read if you're following the **Flight** and **Paint.NET Blaster** tutorials. If you're converting a series of frames, you should make them a numbered sequence, by naming them like so: *Picture000, Picture001, Picture002, Picture003*, and so on. Most animation programs will do this automatically. This ensures the images will import in the correct order.

Make sure your images are in JPG or BMP format, otherwise you may have trouble importing them.

Click *File > Open Files...* and navigate to the folder that contains your images. Select all the images in the animation, and click *Open*. It may take a few minutes for everything to import!

If you numbered everything correctly, you'll be able to play the images back in the order they were captured. Converting them into a video file is simple as following my previous instructions for exporting video files from MPEG Streamclip.

If you have a sequence of images from a DSLR or digital camera, you'll need to perform a few extra steps to ensure your frames are resized correctly. Page ahead to the **Animating with DSLRs** chapter for more instructions.

Trimming, Copying, Pasting & Deleting

If you need to duplicate or remove a section of your animation, this can be done in MPEG Streamclip. See the bar underneath the video file?

Move the slider along the bar until it's resting on the point where you want the edit to start. Tap *I* on the keyboard (short for IN).

To set the end point of the edit, move the slider and hit *O* (short for OUT). The section you've selected will be highlighted, as pictured. Then click *Edit > Trim*, or *Copy*, *Paste*, or *Cut*. These functions are self-explanatory. Sections of video will be pasted where the slider rests on the bar.

Many features and capabilities of MPEG Streamclip were not explored in this brief tutorial. Learn more about this great program by browsing through the help file, and our online tutorials!

Links

MPEG Streamclip (OS X & Windows)

www.squared5.com

Chapter 15

Sharing Your Animations

 ime for the world premiere! Your edit is complete and fans are eager to see your latest film. Successful filmmakers understand it takes hard work and creativity for a film to reach audiences.

Computer Playback

All computers have a media player program that plays audio and video files. Windows programs have **Windows Media Player**. **QuickTime** is installed on Macs, (and Windows too, if you've installed iTunes). If you're into free software, check out **VLC**. These programs are the easiest way to watch animations on the computer they were created on.

Transferring movie files between computers can be complicated. Often files are hundreds of megabytes in size.

Video compression may solve some of these problems, but the recipient's computer still won't be able to play the video file unless the codec you used to compress the video is installed on their computer. For further information about video codecs, read the **Files and Formats** chapter.

It's best to upload the video file to a video sharing site. This allows others to watch and download the movie in a format that works for them.

Video Sharing Sites

Video sharing websites, like YouTube have become tremendously popular. They are currently the best way to distribute short movies to large audiences, with minimal amount of hassle for the viewer and creator.

Kids, ask your parents for permission before visiting video sharing sites, or creating an account on one.

Video uploaded to a website is converted into a format that can be viewed by anyone with a modern web browser, avoiding the codec hassles, large video files, and all the problems that plagued video sharing in the early days of the Internet.

These sites are simple to use. The video creator creates an account and uploads their video file to the website servers, adding a description of the video and keywords that will enable viewers to find the video with search engines.

The server processes the video, converts it into a new format, typically **Flash video (FLV)** and displays the video in the user's profile.

Most video sites have recommended formats and resolutions for uploaded video, and length and file size restrictions too. The website's upload instructions usually have a recommended procedure to follow.

Short Internet videos are the most successful. Expect your viewers to have short attention spans. You'll grab or lose them in the first two seconds.

Releasing films to a public audience entails a knowledge of copyright laws. Most video sharing sites will remove content that is not owned by the uploader.

Making DVDs

DVDs are a great way to distribute easy-to-watch copies of your films. If your computer has a DVD burner, it probably came with a software program that creates finished DVDs. The program should have a step-by-step "wizard" or DVD creation process for you to follow. You provide the video file created by your animation software, or exported from your video editing software. The wizard will do the rest.

Computer to TV

You can easily show your animation to a roomful of people by routing your computer display onto a TV screen. A TV can also be used as a second monitor.

Many laptop computers with DVD players have a **VIDEO OUT** port somewhere. Consult your computer's manual. You may need to visit an electronics retailer or your computer manufacturer to purchase a cable that interfaces with your computer's VIDEO OUT port.

S-Video cables

TVs, DVD players and VCRs have three round connectors. These are called "RCA" or "phono" jacks. The yellow connector is for the video signal, red and white connectors are for audio signals.

S-Video to RCA adapter

"S-Video" connectors are also found in some computers. This is a round connector port with several tiny holes. It may be marked by a picture of a TV screen with a small arrow on it.

If your TV set or DVD player has an S-Video input, you can connect the two with an S-Video cable. If not, you can purchase an "S-Video to Composite" adapter that converts the S-Video plug to an RCA plug.

Audio comes out of your computer's headphone jack. You will need a cable to convert this a 1/8 inch "phone plug," into the red and white "RCA" plugs used by TVs. Or, simply play sound through your computer's speakers.

252

An HDMI port. An (unrelated) FireWire port (1394) is pictured immediately to the right.

If your computer has an HDMI port, and you have an HD-capable TV that accepts HDMI, the two devices can be connected with an HDMI cable.

Copyrights

If you post sound, music, images or video online, or create DVDs and distribute them, ensure you have rights to use the media. This book is not a legal resource, nor is it substitute for advice from a lawyer. However, some great legal resources are available on the web.

- Read books, articles or web sites that explain copyright laws. The Stanford University website has a great introduction to the subject (link at end of chapter)

- Royalty-free music and sound effects can be used in any project after paying a one-time fee.

- If you're a Mac owner, you can compose music with the GarageBand application. You own any music created with the software. Alternatively, perform your own compositions, or ask a talented friend to perform for you.

- Ask a lesser-known non-celebrity artist for permission to use their music in your movie. Sometimes they will say yes, especially if you offer to credit the performer in your film, or a link to their website. Using credited music can be great publicity for them.

- Use Copyleft and Creative Commons licensed materials. Under these licenses, users may copy and create derivative works, if the results are distributed with the same license.

Links

Stanford University: Copyright and Fair Use Explained

fairuse.stanford.edu/Copyright_and_Fair_Use_Overview/index.html

Chapter 16

Animating with DSLRs

 SLR cameras represent the highest-possible image quality achievable by amateur animators. Most theatrical stop motion features today are shot using DSLR cameras, in combination with professional stop motion software.

DSLRs have better optics and sensors than the best webcam or camcorder, and the image files created contain more information than those output by other cameras, which allows the image to be greatly manipulated after filming is complete.

Purchasing a DSLR for stop motion purposes can be bewildering, because so many camera and lens combinations are available. However, I have some recommendations which can help you assemble the needed components, and even save money in the process!

The Sub-$250 DSLR

My goal was to create a DSLR setup for under $250 that could be connected to a computer and used for stop motion work. I succeeded in this quest, however you may want to purchase a newer camera body and different lens if you plan to use the camera for photography outside of stop motion! How was this done? Read on.

The Sub-$250 Stopmotion Explosion DSLR Rig!

Camera: Nikon vs Canon?

Similar to the Mac vs Windows war, camera users battle over whether **Nikon** or **Canon** is the best. Differences between the two may seem very small. Both brands have plenty of lenses and camera bodies to choose from, with similar features at each price point. Anyone who thinks they can tell if a particular picture was taken with a Nikon or Canon camera is kidding themselves. However, there are significant differences between the two brands once you look at the required features for stop motion animation.

When choosing between Nikon and Canon bodies, I checked to see which brand had better support for **tethered shooting**; controlling the camera via USB cable. In particular, I looked for cameras that supported **Live View** mode, which sends an image to the computer, much like a webcam does.

The good news is that both brands have excellent tethering support, and live view is implemented in most new camera bodies. What pushed me towards Canon was the fact that their camera-tethering software is free, whereas Nikon's software has to be purchased separately. This will not make a difference if you are using the camera with third-party stop motion software, but it's one consideration.

Canon implemented live view in their low-end models sooner than Nikon, which means second-hand camera bodies with this feature can be purchased for less. Finally, all of Canon's live view cameras support "exposure simulation", which adjusts the live view video to match the camera settings. Few Nikon cameras have this feature.

I was able to pick up a used Canon EOS Rebel XS body for $119. Even though it's an older model, it still has live view, which is needed in a stop motion DSLR.

Lens: Nikon vs Canon?

You might think that a Canon lens has to be matched with a Canon camera. This is not the case. With an inexpensive lens adaptor, you can attach lenses from many different brands. This opens up a world of possibilities!

Image flicker is a frequently encountered problem when shooting with a DSLR. It can occur even when all auto exposure and white balance controls are disabled, and all lighting problems have been resolved. In these situations, the problem can usually be traced back to the lens being used.

Why is this so? Inside the lens is a component called the "aperture". The aperture works much like the iris of your eye. When your eye sees something bright, the iris closes, limiting the amount of light traveling

Here are two pictures of the same lens. On the left, the aperture is wide open, at the 1.8f setting. On the right, the aperture is closed down to 22f. Remember that the smaller this number (the f-stop), the more open your aperture is, and that more light is reaching your camera sensor.

to your retina. If it becomes dark, the iris opens wide, allowing lots of light inside.

By opening and closing the aperture, you can control the brightness of the image being captured. The aperture also controls how much of the image is in focus, the Depth of Field effect which was introduced in the **Composition** chapter (page 109).

Many cheaper lenses, particularly "kit lenses" which are packaged with DSLR bodies, do not have fully manual aperture control. Instead, the aperture width is set via the camera menu. When an image is taken, the aperture closes to the designated width, then pops open again. This opening and closing of the aperture can be irregular. Tiny variations in width result in images that are slightly darker or brighter. The end result is flickery frames when the animation is played back.

The solution to this problem is using a lens that allows full manual control of the aperture. Fortunately, lenses with this feature are easy to find, and comparatively inexpensive!

The Nikkor Lens

Nikon-brand **Nikkor** lenses are compatible with Nikon cameras all the way back to 1959, thanks to the **Nikon F-Mount** lens connection system. This means that we can use any Nikon F-Mount lens with our Canon camera, as long as we have a Canon-to-F-Mount lens adaptor.

Canon-to-F-Mount lens adaptor.

From left to right, a Nikkor 35-70mm, 50mm and 28mm lens.
All of these would be suitable for stop motion work!

Old Nikkor lenses can be purchased on eBay or occasionally found at yard-sales and flea-markets. For my setup, I purchased a 28mm Nikkor lens for $70 on eBay. Sometimes family members have old film cameras they are no-longer using, the lenses from which would be perfect for stop motion. No matter how old, you can usually google up all the details of a particular lens before purchasing it.

A note regarding the "mm" number. This refers to the focal length of a lens. Lenses with bigger numbers, i.e. a 200-400mm lens are zoom lenses, and are best for sports and wildlife photography. For stop motion, look for lenses in the 28mm to 50mm range.

Some "prime" lenses have a fixed focal length (i.e., a 50mm lens), and cannot be zoomed. A zoom lens will be labeled with two numbers (i.e.,

The image on the left was taken with a 28mm lens, and the image on the right with a 50mm lens.
The camera remained in the same position for both pictures. See how the 28mm lens is "wider" and
shows more, while the 50mm is zoomed in, and shows less. Both lenses would work for stop motion.

a 35-135mm lens), which refers to the minimum and maximum focal length.

The one disadvantage of using older Nikkor lenses with a Canon body, is that you cannot auto-focus the camera. All focus adjustments must be made using the focus ring on the lens. The advantage auto focus gives you, is the ability to adjust the focus of the camera without touching it, via the Canon EOS Utility focus control, or the camera controls in some stop motion software. If you can live without this feature, then using a manual focus lens will not bother you.

Macro Filters

You have a Canon-to-Nikon lens adaptor, and an old Nikkor lens. You'll need one more component to make your lens setup usable. A set of macro lens filters!

Macro filters are like reading glasses, allowing you to focus on objects that are close to the lens. You can buy a complete set of filters for anywhere between $10-15 dollars. Make sure that the filters will fit your camera lens before purchasing a set. Many lenses accept 52mm filters, but not all do.

If you put a 50mm lens on your DSLR and try focusing on a character in your scene, you'll quickly discover that the camera has to be placed a fair distance from the set before the image is in focus, which makes it look like you're shooting a movie from the other end of the block.

Once a macro filter is applied, you can bring the camera lens closer to the action and stay in focus.

No Macro

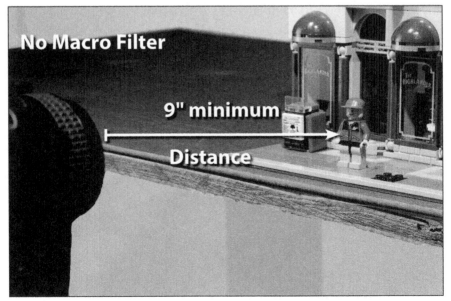

Without a macro filter, the lens has to be at least nine inches away from the set.
Any closer, and the image will be out of focus.

Here are two shots of the same scene with the same lens, except in one setup, I've added a 10x macro filter to the lens, and brought the camera closer. Now the minifig fills the frame!

10x Macro

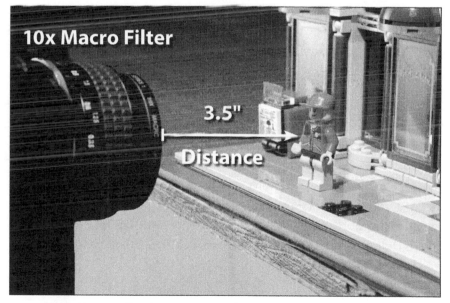

With a 10x macro filter, the camera is 3.5 inches away, and the image is still in focus!

Macro filters typically come in sets with various magnification powers, which can be anywhere between 1x to 10x, depending on the set you purchase. You can even double up filters by screwing them together, but this is usually not required. The higher the magnification, the closer you can bring the lens to the subject.

Using a macro filter increases the depth of field (for a refresher, turn to page 109), which can be a problem since even a slight movement can put a character out of focus. Be prepared to close down the aperture as a countermeasure.

Miscellaneous

It's not a bad idea to purchase a power adaptor, so your camera battery doesn't expire while you're animating. You'll also need a mini USB cable for connecting the camera to your computer, and a tripod. You can use a SD card in the camera, if you wish to simultaneously capture to the camera card and computer.

Software

There are several (commercial) stop motion programs on the market which will connect to, and capture frames from DSLRs directly. If you're using a Canon camera, it's also possible to capture frames with Canon's free **EOS Utility** software.

The drawback of this method is the lack of playback and video-export controls, however you can flip through the frames on your computer using photo-preview software, and convert the frames into video using a frame-conversion program. Because of these limitations, I'd recommend using frame-grabbing software with DSLR connectivity if you're doing complex work. Otherwise, the EOS Utility program is fine for simple animation.

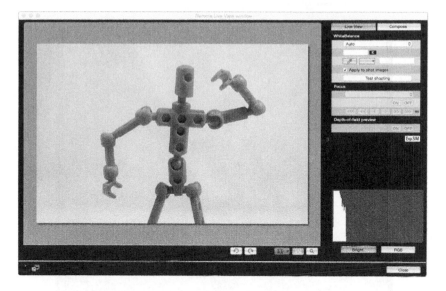

The easiest way to install the EOS Utility program, is via the software CD that is included with all Canon cameras. You can also download it from the Canon website (google "download EOS Utility"), however you will

need your camera's serial number to do so.

After the program is installed and your camera is connected via USB cable, start EOS Utility and select **Remote Shooting** from the startup window.

You'll want to display the **Remote Live View** window as well, so click the **Live View** shoot button.

First, click the folder icon in the main EOS Utility window, and select the folder where you would like to save the images you're capturing.

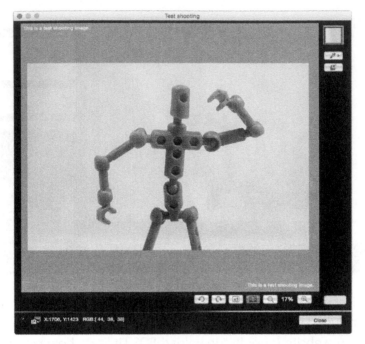

Test Shooting window

Next, in the Live View window, click the ***Test Shooting*** button. Using the capture button in the top-right corner, snap a few pictures and adjust the camera settings until the image looks right. This is necessary, because

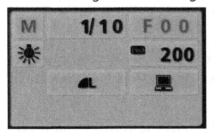

the Live View window ususally does not provide a perfectly accurate preview of the image your camera will capture.

You can adjust the image resolution, shutter speed and ISO settings in the main window. A complete description of these terms is beyond the scope of this book, but as a rule of thumb, higher levels of ISO make the image brighter, but grainer. Faster shutter speeds make the image darker, slower speeds make the image brighter. Try to keep the ISO around 100-400, and the shutter speed between 10-30 tenths of a second.

Also, turn off auto white balance and use a manual setting.

When the test images look good, exit the test window and click the shutter button in the top right corner of the main EOS Utility window. This will capture an image and send it to the computer. A preview window should pop up with the frame you captured. Continue animating and capturing frames.

Since there are no controls to play back the frames, you can open the folder where the frames are being stored, and create a rough preview by starting **Windows Photo Viewer** (right-click the first frame in the sequence and open it with this program) then using the arrows to flip through the frames.

On OS X, use the **Finder Preview.** In the Finder window, click the first image to select it, hit the space bar, and use the arrow keys to flip the frames.

Converting DSLR Frames to Video

To convert your frames into video, you'll use a frame-conversion program, like **MPEG Streamclip.**

After opening your DSLR frames in MPEG Streamclip, and clicking *File > Export...* (choose any video format), you'll see there's an option to crop the output at the bottom of the window. The rest of the settings should match what's pictured on page 268, except for the top and bottom cropping amounts. We need to figure this out first.

If you don't crop the DSLR images during the conversion process, you'll end up with video that looks "squashed". This is due to the DSLR outputting images in a different aspect ratio than the video frame.

How much of the image should be cropped? I've come up with a formula for figuring this out. Sharpen your pencils, or cheat (I'll show you how).

```
                   MPEG Streamclip - MPEG-4 Exporter

Compression:    H.264                                        iTunes...

Quality:                                                     Multipass
50 %                                                         B-Frames

    Limit Data Rate:                    Kbps

Sound:    MPEG-4 AAC         Stereo       Auto        256 kbps

Frame Size:         A professional 2D-FIR   Frame Rate:
                    scaler will be used for
    3456 × 2592 (4:3)       scaling           Frame Blending
    4608 × 2592 (16:9)
    3888 × 2592 (unscaled)                    Better Downscaling
    720 × 576 (DV-PAL)
    720 × 480 (DV-NTSC)                  Deselect for progressive movies:
    1280 × 720 (HDTV 720p)                   Interlaced Scaling
  ● 1920 × 1080 (HDTV 1080i)             ✓ Reinterlace Chroma
    Other:     320  ×  240                    Deinterlace Video

Field Dominance:     Upper Field First       Use "Upper Field First" for all
                                              codecs except DV

Rotation:        No

Zoom:        100   % X/Y    1    Center    0  ,   0

✓ Cropping:     Top  200   Left   0  Bottom 205  Right  0   Source

       Presets...              Reset All              Adjustments...

       Preview        Fast Start          Cancel        Make MP4
```

MPEG Streamclip settings. Make sure the frame rate is correct, Interlaced Scaling is turned off, and you've selected 1920 x 1080 as the frame size. In the crop area, select "Source" in the drop-down menu. For the crop values, keep reading.

First, you'll need to know the ratio of the images that your DSLR is creating. If you don't already know, find the resolution of the image from your DSLR (mine is 3888 x 2592), and calculate the ratio. The easiest way to calculate this is by visiting **Wolfram|Alpha** (**wolframalpha.com**) and typing in the width and height, separated by a colon.

The answer you're looking for is the *"Ratio in lowest terms",* in this case, 3:2. You can keep Wolfram|Alpha open for the next step.

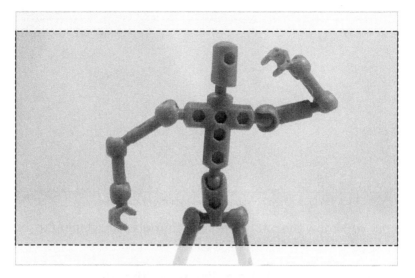

In the top image, you can see that the 3:2 image is a little bit taller than the 16:9 frame. Notice the image area above and below the dotted frame that has been cropped out.

Unless the edges are cropped, the image will be squashed to fit, and appear distorted as in the example below. This is not desirable in most cases.

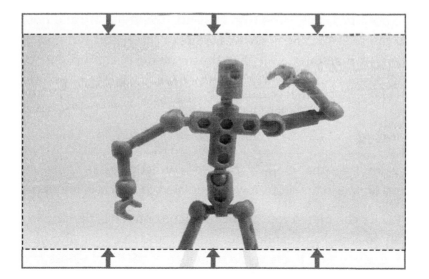

3888:2592

☰ Examples ⤬ Random

Assuming "3888:2592" is referring to math | Use as referring to probabilities instead

Input interpretation:

3888 : 2592

Ratio in lowest terms:

3 : 2

Using WolframAlpha.com to find the ratio in lowest terms

Now that you know the ratio, here's the formula for cropping to 1920 x 1080:

(ImageWidth / X-Ratio) * Y-Ratio - (ImageWidth / (16/9))

Since I have a **3888 x 2592** and **3:2** image, I would enter this into Wolfram|Alpha:

(3888 / 3) * 2 - (3888 / (16/9))

And the answer is **405**! This means I can crop 405 pixels off the top, or 405 off the bottom. I could even crop 200 and 205 off the top and bottom, as you can see I'm doing in the MPEG Streamclip export settings. Using different crop amounts will shift the resulting image up and down slightly, useful if you're trying to improve the composition of your frame.

Zoom: 100 % X/Y 1 Center 0 , 0

☑ Cropping: Top 200 Left 0 Bottom 205 Right 0 Source

To ensure that the crop is applied correctly, make sure you've selected *Source* in the drop-down menu next to the crop amounts.

After you've completed your calculations and entered in the crop values, you can go ahead and export your video. These steps can also be used if someday you wish to convert a sequence of DSLR time-lapse images into a video file.

Chapter 17

What Next?

 nstead of coasting along at a low level of quality or skill, seek to improve your animations by learning new techniques and upgrading your stopmotion studio. Here are some practical suggestions.

Improve Image Quality

A webcam can produce great images, but has its limitations. Higher resolution, better low-light response, even better focus controls can be found in camcorders, and high-end digital still cameras (DSLRs). You can begin your journey towards a better camera setup by gradually acquiring components I recommend in the **Animating with DSLRs** chapter.

Better Lighting

If you've been borrowing the lamp off your parent's desk, drive to an office supply store, visit the lighting aisle, and buy your own desk lamp. Buy some LED bulbs to use in your lights. Remember to avoid bulbs with a wattage higher than what your lamp accepts.

Get a Table

Find a small table you can use for stopmotion and nothing else. This will allow you to leave your animation setups assembled over a period of days, NOT the time between lunch and dinner on the dining room table. For inspiration, check out the picture of the animation setup on page 97. This table was made to be placed on another table, so you can stand while animating.

Become Literary

Improving the content of your films begins with a deeper knowledge of story structure, story genres, and the subject you are presenting. Start writing your stories down in screenplay format. Read books about screenwriting and story beats. Read screenplays, then watch the film based on the screenplay. How does the director translate the screenplay into visual form?

Act with Your Voice

Practice reading stories aloud, giving the characters unique voices. Like a painter uses a brush, the vocal artist creates images with their lungs. Breathing exercises can improve the range and tone of your voice. Here's a simple one.

Breathing Exercise

1. Sit up straight in a chair and look attentive, as if you are gazing at something across the room. Place your hands in your lap, so that your palms rest against your lower abdomen.

2. While sitting like this, breath in slowly and deeply through your nose. Imagine you are filling a balloon, your lungs, to their fullest capacity. Your hands should move out as your lungs fill with air. Keep your chest and shoulders in their normal position as you breath in.

3. After inhaling fully, hold your breath for a moment or two, then exhale slowly through your mouth. Your hands should begin moving in. Concentrate on emptying your lungs from the bottom. Pull your stomach in, tightening your diaphragm muscles. Squeeze every last bit of air from your lungs.

4. Repeat for a few minutes. This exercise will strengthen your abdominal muscles and increase your lung capacity. Your voice will strain less as you have more air and breathing control.

Amp Up Your Audio

Stopmotion is audio-intense. As of this writing, the audio capability of most free video editing software is somewhat limited. To improve the depth and quality of your sound mix, you'll need to invest in pro software, like **Adobe Premiere**, or **Final Cut Pro**. A few of the many programs available are listed in the **Editing** chapter.

Buying better audio recording equipment can also improve your production audio. The **Zoom H1, Zoom H4N** and **Tascam DR-03**, are great pocket recorders and a relatively inexpensive way to record sound anywhere. Get a mic stand, and use a quality pair of headphones, such as the **Sony MDR-V6** to monitor your audio while recording and editing.

Be a Team Player

While stopmotion can be a solitary basement activity, real filmmaking is never a one-man show. Many people come together to create quality works of art. Taking your productions to the next level means drawing from a wider range of talent. Recruit!

Effects

Spice up your films with post-production effects. Use the techniques I described in the **Flight** and **Fighting** chapters to add greater production values to your projects. While it's possible to create believable effects with free software, acquiring a working knowledge of industry standard software, such as **Adobe After Effects**, is a marketable skill, and might land you a job someday.

Moving On

If you find stopmotion fun, but want to start creating traditional movies in the real world, you can purchase a camera, audio equipment, and basic lighting package. Some investments you've made in software and stopmotion skills will follow you into the new medium, some will not.

Editing

In stopmotion, it's possible stretch the footage you have as far as it will possibly go, recycling and re-arranging frames like a miser. In live-action video, you record far more footage than is used in the final film. Working with a surplus of footage may be bewildering at first. Much of your time editing will be spent trimming long sections of video into small individual clips.

Sound

Audio recorded outside of a quiet room can be very messy. The best results are achieved with a second microphone, which can be held close to the subject being recorded. You are rarely close enough to record audio with the camera's onboard microphone!

Lighting

Three-point lighting techniques are used in stopmotion and real-world applications, but the equipment becomes much larger and heaver. Dealing with the sun and clouds is a constant battle (which animators conveniently avoid in their basement studios).

Cameras

Recording to a MiniDV tape or flash card and downloading the footage to your computer may seem novel after saving your footage to the computer directly. The camera's control menus will share some settings found in your webcam's image controls. Techniques such as **rack focus** (when the camera's focus moves between  two objects in a shot), **tilts** (tilting the camera up and down) and **pans** (panning the camera left and right) are much easier to apply while the camera is rolling, rather than performing the movement one frame at a time.

Invest in a tripod, but don't be afraid to move the camera off the tripod and around the room between shots, searching for good composition, locking the camera down again when a good frame is found.

An in-depth coverage of video cameras and their features is beyond the scope of this book; however, I encourage you to look for a camera in the "prosumer" range that accepts external audio inputs.

In Conclusion

Whatever films you create, think about them not as simple exercises, or random artistic doodles but as expressions of your beliefs.

Become excellent at your craft.

Avoid triviality and mediocrity.

Use your skill for good. And importantly...

Have Fun!

Special Thanks To:

Amanda, Becky, Emily, Mark, Nathaniel, Rebekah, Rob, Robbie, and Ryan

Index

A

D

E

T

U

V

W